WHO
is the new
HOW

JUSTIN PALMER
AND JESSICA SCHERTZ

FOREWORD BY **ALEX MORGAN**, WORLD CUP CHAMPION AND OLYMPIC GOLD MEDALIST

WHO
is the new
HOW

STRATEGIES TO
FIND, RECRUIT, AND CREATE
THE BEST TEAMS

WILEY

For general information on our other products and services or for technical support, please contact our Customer Care Department within the United States at (800) 762-2974, outside the United States at (317) 572-3993 or fax (317) 572-4002.

Wiley also publishes its books in a variety of electronic formats. Some content that appears in print may not be available in electronic formats. For more information about Wiley products, visit our web site at www.wiley.com.

Library of Congress Cataloging-in-Publication Data is Available:

ISBN: 9781119898986 (Cloth)
ISBN: 9781119899075 (ePub)
ISBN: 9781119899082 (ePDF)

Cover Design: Paul McCarthy
SKY10046685_042823

Contents

Contents

Foreword

Teams are something I'm incredibly familiar with—I've been on them for most of my life. They've been a source of strength, pride, comfort, and growth for me, and I've taken my role on them very seriously—not only because I've experienced the value of a good teammate more times than I can count, but because I know that a team is only as effective as the individuals on it. Each member must show up every day, armed with the diverse ways they alone can contribute to the success of the team.

Finding those people—the elusive right fit—can be difficult. If you think of it in the context of a professional soccer team, it's not about just finding the person who can kick the soccer ball the best. You need one (or ten) of those of course, but there are so many other things that need to be taken into consideration. Each position calls for specific strengths, from physical skills to mental disposition. Each player needs a competitive yet compatible edge that contributes to on-the-field dynamics and locker room camaraderie. Each team member—coaches, support staff, comms team, front office, game day ops, volunteers—relies on their counterparts to execute duties in accordance with the larger goal. The success of each game is dependent on how effectively all those factors work together.

This type of teamwork is integral in both sports and business. They appear as two different landscapes, but they both entail high stress and mentally demanding situations. They both rely on consistency, communication, and making smart decisions. They both hope to attain peak performance through planning, executing, implementing, and monitoring. They both come down to the caliber and dynamic of the people on the team.

My experience on teams and my knowledge of their intricacies is what led me to partner with Teamable. At the onset, I was drawn to their mission: build teams with strength and purpose. But it was the intention underneath the mission that really resonated with me. They want to transform lives by connecting candidates to roles that fulfill both them and their companies. These aren't just fluffy words; they're a sign that Teamable is in tune with the current disenchantment of the workforce and knows the true value of the right people being in the right roles at the right companies. And perhaps most importantly, they know it requires a recruiting approach that's equal parts methodical and empathetic.

I've spent time with Justin Palmer and Jessica Schertz, Teamable's CEO and COO, and they care as deeply as I do about teams, community, building, fulfillment, finding your people, and finding your calling. Accordingly, everything Teamable does is built upon those foundations. They take into account all the small details that make up the whole of a candidate, as well as all the facets of a company—what it does, how it's run, and what type of person would excel there—and bring them together. They see it as finding the perfect piece of the puzzle for a company, rather than just filling an open role within a short amount of time or prioritizing counterproductive metrics like "time-to-fill." It's about far more than that and their incredible product, work culture, happy customers, and results show it.

As Teamable's new Chief Inspiration Officer, I'm so excited to be part of the company and continue to lend my expertise on what it really takes to build the best teams possible. This book is a perfect entry point to get familiar with all the things that go into that. It will challenge you to rethink who you're actually looking for, how you're going to find them, and what it can mean for both the candidate's and company's fulfillment if you do. But most of all, it will show you the infinite value of filling a team with the right people. When you do, they'll be an unstoppable force.

—Alex Morgan

Introduction

We believe that something is wrong with the way we're all working. And in 2017, we founded Teamable in order to fix it.

In today's world, the *what* and *how* often drive product and company growth. Successful brands have strong missions and clear business development strategies; they know exactly what they're aiming to accomplish and how they're going about it. But there's something far more significant that makes it all possible, something that gives those brands the competence, momentum, scalability, and execution they need to achieve long-term success: the *who*.

This isn't a revolutionary insight. Every employer knows how important it is to have a capable, talented team of people working for them. Every team member knows how productive and invigorating it is when they're working with the right blend of people. Every recruiter knows how valuable it is to find the superstars who will perfectly round out a team. But here's what everyone doesn't seem to know: traditional recruitment practices aren't cutting it.

Recruitment today is so similar to how it was 100 years ago. Employers want candidates based on specific criteria and recruiters source people who meet them. While the ways in which recruiters go about the sourcing has changed—insofar as technology has made it more convenient—they're still pressed for time and competing for the same pool of candidates as everyone else. To add to the chaos, they're now also drowning in recruitment tools. But is it working?

If you're holding this book, you know it's not.

We reached the same conclusion just prior to founding Teamable. But before we go any further, we want to introduce you to who we are. This book is written by two of us: Justin Palmer and Jessica Schertz, CEO and COO of Teamable, respectively. While the book is penned as one voice, we'll briefly deviate here so you get to know who you're hearing from.

I'm Justin, and my road to working on Teamable wasn't obvious at the time, but it is now.

My career started as a technologist first. I studied computer science for about five years, dropped out of a PhD program, and worked as a researcher and engineer working on AI and human language for over a decade. I fell in love with the idea that you could build software systems that learn to do things people can do, and I haven't looked back.

To make progress in that field takes a ton of different skill sets, and so I spent the better part of 15 years training up. I had so many great mentors along the way who taught me about building great software, managing data, setting up good experiments, the math behind modern AI, and so much more. That's the super short version of the technologist in me. I talk about some of that later in this book.

What gets me excited about technology is simple: it's the opportunity for impact. If you build systems that deal with even small language problems, that helps people communicate and make sense of ideas at a scale only made possible by technology. It redefines the limits of human ability and creativity. But it wasn't until I moved to Silicon Valley that I came to understand that there are equally impactful opportunities to do the same thing in business, and that happens through building technology companies.

My first job in the Valley was at LendingHome. We wanted to reinvent the mortgage bank and it was a crash course in a lot of things. I learned all about how mortgage finance and the capital markets work. I came to understand how all kinds of stuff from my days in natural language processing applied to the way people think about predicting how mortgages and financial markets perform. Our team grew from the first five of us, sitting around a single table in the same room where Uber started, to a team of over 250 in two years. We became the number one lender for home investor loans in the United States. I loved it. But it was building the company, and the team side of things, that struck me. We all worked so hard and did all of this because of each other. It wouldn't have been possible any other way. I met people who had spent most of their careers doing marketing, mortgage, or finance and we worked together to make each other better. I saw how much impact a diverse team could have when working together on a hard problem.

So when starting Teamable, I didn't fully appreciate it at the time, but it was a similar motivation that got me started and has kept me excited. We started out doing recruiting. I got to know an awesome person named Teresa and helped her find a new job that she still has today. She and I still talk every so often. Ask any recruiter, and they'll tell you the first person they helped find a new role. Everyone who's done this remembers the first person we helped get hired, and when it works, they remember us too. It's an amazing feeling.

That's how our company started. By doing some recruiting then figuring out how technology fit in. We felt the pain firsthand and wanted to create a good solution. So we knew exactly what to build in order to help anyone work like the best recruiters, but also with technology at the heart of it.

Our team still works this way, and so do I. We always acknowledge that the crux of our work is people and software coming together to get things done. When you add people to part of what you're building, it opens new doors. We have always done that, and it makes all the difference. It pushes the limits of how we think about what's possible, so we're always forward-thinking as technologists. We stay rooted in the day-to-day of what our customers do, so that we get better in ways that are really direct. It also means our entire team works together without silos, and that is what makes us build special things.

The more we grow, the more we want to do, and the more excited I get. Finding a job, or your next teammate, has changed some in the last 70 years but so much hasn't. We know that technology hasn't really transformed this space yet, and we're changing that. Our motivation is why we got here, and our mission is growing.

We're writing this because we want to share how we think about that mission. This book is about what we've learned so far, what we plan to do, and our motivation. It's about the stories we love of amazing teams that inspire us. We teamed up with Alex Morgan because she's one of those people. She is an awesome athlete, a force in sports, and has transformed how we think. She's a team builder and like so many people we find inspiring and feature in this book, Alex plays the long game and wants to change how the world works. We want to make a similar impact as a company, and we're honored to be part of that story.

Hi, I'm Jessica. As a lover of data and problem solving, I joined Teamable in its earliest days. My role morphed from the one-person Operations team to the Head of Operations who oversaw dozens of people. I then became the Chief of Staff to have a broader impact on all parts of the business, before my focus kept naturally returning to all things operations and I became Teamable's COO.

I never thought I'd be a COO. After studying Public Health in college, I went to law school and then got my master's degree in Education, focusing on English Language Learners (ELL). I started volunteering a lot with refugees, teaching ELL classes and helping them get their bearings once they started to build a life in my community. I absolutely loved the work. I felt like I'd been set on fire—I was so excited, so passionate, and so driven by seeing the students thrive. It was my first glimpse into what fulfilling work was all about. And if you know, you know. It's that stop-at-nothing, keep-you-up-at-night, what-I'm-doing-matters feeling.

That's when a former colleague of Justin's reached out to me for help with some work. It was a lot of the same types of problems that early-stage Teamable was working on—weird little natural language processing problems, human-in-the-loop, AI, etc. And it was really interesting to me from a language standpoint. It felt like the same approach I'd used to teach English to a room full of people who all had a different native language. Except this time, it was communicating with a robot, essentially. And trying to find a way for us to understand each other just as I'd tried to achieve with a student.

I became obsessed with the work. I had no idea that my output was ten times more than any other contributor's because I was just focused on getting my hands on more projects and cracking the code and figuring out how to make it work. There was a brilliant engineer named Dima, Teamable's future CTO, working on the same project and when Justin wanted to build a recruitment platform that used a similar approach, he contacted Dima and me to see if we were interested. We both jumped at the chance.

I thought it would be temporary. But as the series of really interesting problems emerged, I got more and more hooked. As soon as we'd solved one, there would be something else that caught my attention that I wanted to rip apart and figure out. I remember wearing out the button on my wireless mouse in the middle of the night because I was just constantly cranking on those weird little problems for hours and hours every day.

I brought in some other people—most of whom still work with us, shout-out to Bruce, Jared, Joe, and Ray!—and informally ran that team for about a year. We would meet in San Francisco and geek out about what we were building (which was a very basic version of what we have today). I learned sourcing so I could focus on improving the sourcing technology we were developing. We built the dictionary that our AI uses to speak to candidates about their backgrounds. I took an early stab at what is now Flex, our full-cycle recruiting, by taking a crash course in recruiting and jumping into the task of finding candidates with top-secret security clearance or experience building autonomous vehicles. I learned as much as I could about what makes start-ups work and about all of the dysfunctional pieces that make them flop.

Our motto was very much "say yes and figure it out later." We were a whole team of people who were completely obsessed with seeing where we could push this thing. There were a lot of all-nighters that never felt like working. We'd get on Zoom (I guess it was just Google Meet back then) and work until the middle of the night because we all cared about being able to deliver our product to our customer list—which was growing exponentially—and we cared about each other and didn't want to flake on anyone (we always used the analogy of rowing together; when everyone is paddling, you zoom through the water and it isn't hard work, but if someone drops their oars, everyone else has to pick up the slack . . . no one wanted to be the one to drop the oars). In those days, the most senior employees would jump in and do the most basic work of the whole product, either because it needed to be done to keep things moving or because it was crucial that everyone understood every piece of the product. No one was above anything, and no one was below it, either.

The "fulfillment at work" stuff is so important to me because I've lived it. Early in my college and career days, it was peak "Lean In" era and I never really connected with that message. It didn't feel like progress to me. I didn't like the message that women can "have it all," and any failure to do so is on them to fix.

Between the backlash from that movement and also what's happened post-COVID, I don't think people are buying into that anymore. I don't think any adult (especially a woman and *especially* a mom) thinks they can really have it all. We will always be dropping some kind of ball and, particularly in tech, the second you feel you've got it figured out, you'll need to pivot. And fast. I guess we could find a job that lets us coast—we can sit on our couch and watch Netflix while making sure to jiggle the mouse every five minutes so it looks like we're active. But most people don't want that. We want our lives to be full of things we're thrilled to be doing.

When we're trying to juggle everything in our lives, it can be completely draining if we don't love those pieces. Life is short and the juggling act is hard, and people are now feeling like they don't want to make huge concessions anymore. That's not to say we shouldn't try to create change. Of course we should. I've hired a ton of women—moms, digital nomads, transitioning teachers. I was the only woman on the team when I joined, and for quite a while after. Now we're over 50% female. Creating that environment doesn't fully protect me from the yuckiness—like joining a call and the person on the other end just assumes I'm there to take notes (ouch) or having men mansplain to me why there aren't more women in tech. I would never say that employees should just abandon ship if their workplace doesn't reflect their ideal. I'm saying that all of the work we need to do—make the workplace more equitable, earn a living while also raising a family and having a life, build a product that helps people do more of what they care about—means we *have* to be doing that work for something we feel connected to. And it has to be done with a team we know is rooting us on.

We have an incredible team who feels that same way. Some have gone to top schools, live in the Bay Area, and fit that stereotypical image of someone who brings value in tech. But some of our biggest wins are thanks to people who took unconventional paths; people who pull from their unique experiences and are totally into the work they're doing. People do really big, exciting, impactful work when they're surrounded by people who share their mission. Though where the discussion goes south is when that's treated as a novelty. Conversations around moms returning to the workforce or hiring veterans or other underrepresented groups are usually framed as doing those candidates a favor. They're hired "even though . . ." or because a company's making concessions just so they can fill a quota. Neither of those is true.

The story here is not how remarkable it is that a former stay-at-home mom from rural Illinois with some weird degrees is an executive at a tech company. Or that we hired a freelance writer who was living in Argentina because he'd fallen in love with a girl he met while traveling through, and now five years later he's our best account manager and knows every piece of the product because he helped build it from scratch. The real story is all the people who are passed over who would really dig into a mission and get stuff done, all because people didn't think about the problem in the right way and find a solution that actually solved it.

That's what we've built at Teamable: a solution. We believe businesses thrive when work is a source of fulfillment for employees. In fact, we know it. So our solution optimizes every step of the hiring process. Our end-to-end software, supported by expert guidance, empowers talent professionals to find top performers, connect them with fulfilling work, and drive business growth as a result.

This book isn't a way for us to sell you a product. This book is an agglomeration of what we've seen, heard, and encountered in the recruitment industry. It's full of facts, insights, and stories about the gaps in recruiting, the direct consequences of those gaps, and what it could mean for the workforce and workplace if the gaps are properly filled. This book is divided into three strategies, all of which urge you to rethink something: who you're actually looking for, how you're going to go about finding them, and what it could mean for your team's morale and success if you do. The chapters therein explore why the rethinking is necessary and reiterate that although the *what* and *how* are the backbone of any business model, the secret of success is all about the *who*.

More than anything, we hope this book proves the indisputable value of connecting the right candidates with the right companies to create the right teams. The best teams. The ones that aren't settling for a less-than–perfect fit or toiling away on unfulfilling work. Because employees and companies both deserve better.

Rethink Who You're Looking For

1 | A Matter of Intention

In Silicon Valley, venture capitalists love to use certain key phrases. When it comes to people, there's one to describe the typical founder that always stuck with us: central casting. A founder that comes out of central casting went to the right school, worked at the right company, presents with the right level of polish, and is a polymath of sorts—did something artsy to go with their love of technology, for example. Stanford or MIT computer science, then on to Dropbox or wherever, then broke out to do their next thing. It works, so the story goes, because it is the people-version of a more general phrase that dominates thinking: pattern matching.

The only problem is, pattern matching works until it doesn't. The best companies, and the best teams, are most successful when they do more than match a pattern. Innovation, almost by definition, isn't about matching templates.

People who build the next best thing have to be in it for more. They have to love what they do. They've got to be all in for what they want to build as ambitious people who crave impact. The company we keep is just group of people. And to build a meaningful company, it takes a team. People who crave impact, who aren't just looking to copy and paste, match a pattern, play a part. Sure, there's no sense in reinventing the wheel every time, but there has to be more to how we approach things. Curiosity, ingenuity, creativity.

People who build amazing things work together as an amazing team. They are groups of people who look to each other to make an impact, do something cool, and have fun along the way.

And of course, the best VCs know this, and are careful not to pattern match too aggressively. They know the best teams might have some things in common, but outliers are outliers, and so there will always be something unique about a great team on a great mission. When you pull from central casting, you outsource thinking about the right team to a template. You give up on looking more closely and going deeper.

There are so many examples where central casting didn't work. But let's talk about a famous one: Quibi.

When Quibi launched in April 2020, it seemed destined to succeed. The new streaming platform, which generated 10-minute episodes of original content to be viewed on smartphones, targeted users with short attention spans and filled its initial 50-show roster with A-listers from Dwayne "The Rock" Johnson to the Kardashians. It rose to No. 3 in Apple's App Store on its first day, had 1.7 million downloads in its first week, and was the 11th most downloaded app of the month.[1] The numbers were lower than they hoped—but on paper, it was a success.

Quibi was the brainchild of Jeffrey Katzenberg, for whom success was nothing new. As the former Disney studio head and DreamWorks cofounder, his accomplishments in the entertainment industry were formidable: reviving Disney's animation business with hits like *Little Mermaid* and *Beauty and the Beast*, overseeing DreamWorks Animation for no fewer than 30 films, winning an Academy Award, and accumulating a net worth of $880 million. Given his credible track record and deep connections, investors jumped at the chance to back his newest venture. Huge entities like Goldman Sachs, Alibaba, Madrone Capital, and every major studio, from Disney to 21st Century Fox to

Sony, helped Quibi amass a total of $1.75 billion in funding.[2] And to further secure Quibi's success, Katzenberg recruited Meg Whitman to come aboard as CEO.

For nearly two decades, Whitman had been one of Silicon Valley's heaviest hitters, growing eBay from 30 to 15,000 employees and $4 million to $8 billion in revenue.[3] Later, she revived Hewlett-Packard, then the largest tech company in the world, after its stock dropped 46% the preceding year.[4] Spanning her career were high-level positions at Procter & Gamble, The Walt Disney Company, and Stride Rite Corporation, along with prominent political activity, including a 2010 run for governor of California. Whitman's resume was impressive, indeed. With her and Katzenberg at the helm of the new mobile-video app, Quibi was a new entertainment company founded, literally, out of central casting. The best in entertainment and the best in business joined forces to start an entertainment business. There was no way it could fail.

Until it did.

Just six months after Quibi went live, the team announced it was shutting down. Katzenberg and Whitman cited an array of contributing factors: the COVID-19 pandemic, market saturation, ongoing lawsuits over the app's Turnstyle technology, and, according to an open letter to Quibi's employees, investors, and partners, "because the idea itself wasn't strong enough to justify a standalone streaming service."[5]

While these are all valid factors, there's one thing they neglected to mention: sometimes the best person on paper isn't the best person for the job. It's hard to put a script to how the most successful businesses come to be. And businesses and companies are groups of people working toward a goal. They are all about having the right people, but also the right goals. Quibi was a tech company without a technologist at the helm.

Katzenberg and Whitman brought to the table a laundry list of individual achievements and combined decades of experience in Hollywood and Silicon Valley. They were experts on global expansion, mergers and acquisitions, and organizational restructuring. They knew their way around board rooms, press conferences, and stock reports. They had had proven success with resurrecting companies, reviving brands, and raising capital. In short, they were clearly qualified to run a company. But were they the *right* ones to run Quibi? They helped many global businesses grow, but not start. They were entrepreneurial and commercial, but they were not technologists. They tried to apply known playbooks and people who looked great on paper—to start something entirely different. They started by thinking like a big company first, not the upstart they were. They needed something that wasn't in their DNA.

Entertainment was Katzenberg's passion. His years at Paramount, Disney, and DreamWorks showed that he was great at taking a known thing—in this case, movie production—and improving it. But since Quibi was actually a technical endeavor, it had different economies of scale, different personalities that needed to come together, different consumer behavior. So in order to be successful, it called for a different skill set, a different fundamental look at businesses, a different style of working. A different type of person.

Whitman's past successes were in e-commerce and tangible goods. Plenty of people industry hop and find their footing, but the colossal undertaking that was Quibi was ripe for someone with an inherent comprehension of the market, product, and audience.

Industry proficiency aside, Katzenberg and Whitman's shared understanding (or lack thereof) of Quibi's value proposition and distinctive capabilities was the real tipping point. Despite the fact that both were in their 60s and not very active on social media, they believed they had unique insight into which user experience, features, engagement modes, content, and technology would appeal to young consumers, plus a handle on how to target them. In reality, they were out-of-touch with how to create and market a modern platform for the millennial generation. They didn't understand it would start with technology rather than entertainment. TikTok and Instagram didn't start as media companies. YouTube started as a way for people to publish their own home videos. Of course, all three platforms now provide this, but they've branched into something their founders could never have imagined. They're entirely new media platforms of their own, not remixes of existing things.

It's easy to oversimplify the issues that plagued Quibi—which were numerous and justified—by isolating the shortcomings of executive leadership. But we do so to point out the importance of placing the right people, with backgrounds and mindsets that are perfect fits for the company, in the right roles.

What would have happened had Katzenberg honestly determined the needs of the company and done his due diligence to find a partner whose aptitudes aligned with them? What if Katzenberg had gotten out of his own way and relied on the employees and advisors at Quibi, many of whom were proficient in technology, entertainment, market research, UI/UX, and millennial behavior? What if neither was hands-on, and just focused on hiring other leaders who were technologists first? Would that have led to alternative decision making and goals? What would have been top of mind for the team looking to its leaders for how to operate?

We'll never know.

Hiring someone is almost always a gamble; they either turn out to be a tremendous asset for an organization or slow both the company and their team down if they're not a good match. In today's competitive market, utilizing new and effective methods to find top candidates can mean the difference between the two.

We believe hiring is most effective when it connects companies and candidates with matching trajectories who fulfill one another's particular needs. When we talk about the company we keep, we use the same word to describe the place we work: company. It's very telling. The shared trajectory and values have to be aligned, but we have to be complementary. Some things cannot be compromised: values, goals, work ethic. And those are intrinsic to what motivates us. But we all have distinct interests and skills. When it all works best is when those interests come together, in the form of different people with diverse interests, to form a great company. Companies work best when each teammate makes the whole group better. The team does something no individual can. There are a million cliches about this (the whole and the sum of parts thing), but it's true, and it's what good teams all have in common.

But great teams also have something else. They need intangibles. Intrinsic motivation that can't be stopped. A mission they're pumped about. Ambitious goals that they want to see come to life in the world. They need a Goldilocks sort of balance between structure that gives them guidance about what to do, and how they fit into the organization. But they also need the deeper direction to do it in a way where they add the most they can. When people are at their best, they don't just take a job—they make it their own.

Whether finding teammates via structured means or basing it off more collective intel to gauge potential, it all starts with getting real about what you want to achieve and then finding the type of person who's best suited to help you get there. You want team building to be a process that gets you a company all of its own, too.

A Brief History of Standards

The Roman army in the fourth century B.C. had stringent criteria for prospective soldiers: they had to be Roman citizens, capable of marching 20 miles while wearing the full uniform, armor, and weapons; able to carry 60 pounds of supplies; and have "unwavering discipline and patriotism."[6] What's more, due to laws imposed by the Roman Senate, a citizen could not be hired into just any position. Roman society was divided into five classes that determined where one could work in the army, with the wealthiest—the first class— most heavily armed and equipped with helmets, armor, spears, and swords. The lower classes bore less protection and weaponry; the fifth class carried no armor at all and was armed with only slings.

Two thousand years later, little seems to have changed. We've come a long way from the archaic requirements that were once used to source potential soldiers, but requirements exist just the same. Social hierarchy still impacts certain groups over others. And while major technical advancements have changed the way we find, organize, track, and reach candidates, it has not fundamentally changed how we recruit. We still look to "check the boxes." We talk about job "requirements." Of course, requiring someone to be able to do the work is important and critical. But we can easily get carried away. Listing job requirements is often as aspirational as it is pragmatic.

With a working-age population of over 214 million in the United States alone,[7] the amount of potential talent is staggering. Yet according to a recent Recruiter Sentiment Study, 63% of recruiters said the barrier to identifying qualified talent was not finding enough suitable candidates.[8] "Suitable" is of course subjective, and its meaning depends on the prerequisites set forth by the employer. These are really a reflection of what all might need to get done (e.g., a long list of requirements), and a transliteration of skills that are hard to measure (e.g., skill) into ones that are not (e.g., years of experience).

Prerequisites are the first line of defense in the recruitment process, and understandably so; employers want to ensure applicants have what they're looking for, and job seekers want to determine if they're suitable for the role before applying. It gives some rough parameters to everyone interested in the conversation. The most common prerequisites we see today won't surprise you: education, job history (which encompasses work titles, duties, and length of time at the company), location, and diversity. But often it leads to judgment too quickly.

The goal of a recruiting conversation should not be to arrive at yes or no as quickly as possible; for many roles, it's much better for the goal to be reciprocal. If there's a job and a candidate that seems like a pretty good fit, before getting rigid, consider that they just might be. The candidate and company should tell each other their story and figure it out. Hiring is less like a puzzle that needs all the pieces to fit together than it is an orchestra looking for its magic musician. Of course, this isn't always the case; sometimes you'll just need someone who can do a particular job really, really well. But if a person is going to transform a company, they will make the job their own and run with it, in an inspired way. There is more involved in sussing out how someone will do the job; how they work, learn, and collaborate are full of intangibles. Most successful people do well on these dimensions, none of which fits neatly on a résumé.

With the expectation of a college degree for a range of roles, one can presume employers want candidates with specialized knowledge about a particular career or industry. It's not unreasonable to want to fill high-ranking finance positions, for example, with people who have an accredited understanding of financial modeling, macro- and microeconomics, and portfolio management.

Two decades ago, companies began adding degree requirements to job descriptions that hadn't previously needed them, even though the jobs themselves hadn't changed. This widespread phenomenon was referred to as "degree inflation" and became particularly pronounced after the Great Recession. Degrees themselves got more specialized, and we saw even more universities pop up to address the demand. From 2010 to 2019, using a college degree as a proxy for job competency and career readiness immediately eliminated 64% of working-aged adults who did not hold a four-year degree.[9]

Today, a growing number of companies, including many in tech, are dropping the requirement for a bachelor's degree for many middle-skill and even higher-skill roles in favor of skills-based hiring. As for the roles that necessitate a degree, some employers have broadened their parameters, such as by recruiting candidates from an array of accredited colleges, not just top-tier universities. That shift, set in motion prior to 2020 but most certainly accelerated by the Covid-19 pandemic labor shortage, has widened the talent pool by removing barriers to entry.

The call for past job titles and work experience follows a similar logic; when candidates have a background in specific roles or functions, it can ensure the right levels of context around what they will be doing. Their responsibilities and capabilities will be well matched.

If an agency is looking for an ad executive, a candidate's history of being a brand manager who successfully executed large-scale campaigns takes the guesswork out of their competency.

The pronounced importance of titles and experience requirements came courtesy of *The Dictionary of Occupational Titles* in 1938. Produced by the US Department of Labor for employers, government officials, and workforce development professionals, this roster of job descriptions defined over 13,000 types of work and detailed the skills, knowledge, and experience needed for someone to succeed in the role.[10] It was replaced in 1997 by an online equivalent, though much of the content has remained unchanged.

As years pass and economies shift, so do the creation of new jobs, in both title and scope. Where familiar job titles like executive, associate, specialist, and expert were once the norm, they're increasingly being augmented with more levels and specialization. Microsoft has nine levels of software engineering talent, across dozens of disciplines. To some degree, specialization is important as it increases excellence. But as times change, so will skills and titles. People who keep pace with the change, for example, won't have such specialized titles. Software engineers that are "full stack" are generalists who know enough to do a few things well. Ironically enough, they may be disqualified from something they do exceptionally well, because of the general title. It is a strange situation.

People make up for this by falling back on a profile's explanation of duties as it pertains to a specific role, though that comes with its own worries. A recent study published in *Harvard Business Review* investigated the link between an employee's prior work experience and their performance in a new organization and found no significant correlation between the two. Even when people had completed tasks, held roles, or worked in functions or industries relevant to their current ones, it didn't translate into better performance.[11] You're likely as surprised as we were because this goes against the logical and long-held assumption that people with experience, especially directly relevant experience, would outperform those without it.

The study's coauthors speculate a possible reason for the discrepancy, noting that many measures of experience are pretty basic: the number of jobs held, tenure at previous employers, years of total work. While those metrics indicate whether a candidate possesses experience, they don't speak to the quality or significance of that experience, which would have more bearing on performance.

Diversity is a more recent addition to the requirements our clients set. In a world where companies are increasingly judged by their commitment to diversity, that commitment is shown most visibly by the racial and ethnic diversity present (or not) in the pool of candidates being hired and promoted. Despite the Civil Rights Act of 1964 banning workplace discrimination on the basis of race, sex, religion, and national origin, it's the more recent movements, such as Black Lives Matter, that led many companies to prioritize recruiting people of various ethnicities.

A recent report from McKinsey & Company shows how having a diverse workforce isn't just politically correct, it's smart business. Over the course of five years, researchers tracked the progress of over 1,000 companies in 15 countries across 17 industries and found that companies in the top quartile for ethnic diversity are 12% more likely to outperform all other companies in the data set. What's more, they also found that companies with female executive-team representation exceeding 30% are significantly more likely to outperform those whose executive teams are 10–30% female. Those companies, in turn, are more likely to outperform those with fewer than 10% female executive-team representation. As a result, there is a substantial likelihood of an outperformance differential—48%—between the most and least gender-diverse companies.[12]

From as far back as 1920, when the US Department of Labor added a Women's Bureau to foster more career opportunities for women, the female population has been fighting to prove their worth in the workplace. The rise of social movements like #MeToo and well-publicized examples of women in executive leadership—from Katharine Graham becoming the first CEO of a Fortune 500 company in 1972 to Kamala Harris being named the first female US vice president in 2020—has steadily progressed women's presence in the workforce. In 2022, the employment-population ratio for women was 54.4%, compared to 30.9% in 1948.[13]

Our own data shows promise but opportunity: in 2020, our tech clients contacted mostly male engineers, with women making up just 24% of the outreaches; analyst positions were split between 60% men to 40% women; and product managers roles saw men account for 58% of the sourced candidates. In contrast, it is in nontechnical roles where we've seen women have the upper hand: in marketing, women made up 55% of the outreaches; for both recruiting and accounting positions, our clients contacted 66% women.

There are numerous other prerequisites set by our clients for sourcing candidates, but those preceding are often deemed most important. The assumption is that if all these stipulations are in place, effectively filtering out those who don't qualify, the perfect candidate will emerge.

And sometimes they do.

When It All Goes Right

When Figma's sales needed a nudge two years after its public release, the browser-based interface design tool had one million users and a revenue of $3 million.[14] They wanted to increase their metrics across the board, so advisors told Figma cofounder and CEO Dylan Field that he better start looking for an effective head of marketing.

John Lilly, one of Figma's board members and a partner at VC firm Greylock, used our software to help reach candidates. He found Amanda Kleha. With a BA in business administration from the University of Washington and an MBA from Yale School of Management, Kleha worked as a product marketing manager for Google's Enterprise SaaS businesses before joining the marketing team at software company Zendesk, where she worked her way up to senior vice president of marketing and sales strategy.

Her seven-year stretch at Zendesk saw the company make an IPO, grow from 12 to 2,000 employees, expand from 1,000 to 3,000 customers, and go from $1 million to $300 million in revenue.[15] She had a proven history of using data to make educated decisions, and was passionate about brand building, user experience, customer service, online metrics, and finding and nurturing great talent.

Could she be the one? Lilly had saddled his search with stringent requirements, all of which Kleha met, but he knew the difference between being qualified for a role and having the strengths that aligned with a company's purpose and goals.

Lilly and Field were hopeful and excited when they sat down to meet with her, but she seemed hesitant. Kleha had just left her role at Zendesk and was enjoying life, reveling in the newfound freedom of not having to set an alarm clock. They pitched her anyway, explaining their need for someone to help increase Figma's product sales through expanding their sales division and bolstering customer service.

Her response was as customer-focused as theirs was growth-focused.

"What would the customer want you to do? It's easy to talk about what's right for the business, what's easy to do on a roadmap, what resources you have . . . and it's really easy to turn your back on what matters: your customer and what's right for them."[16]

She went on to explain some of the lessons she'd learned at Zendesk, refuting the traditional approach. Zendesk ended up having seven sales segments at one point and Kleha thought that made it really complicated for not a lot of benefit. The company had also created both a success team and a management team, which she felt muddied the water for the customer as to who owned the relationship. With a product like Figma, there wasn't a lot to set up; it was a pretty easy product to start using right away. If they could keep things really simple for as long as possible, she felt it would benefit them in the long run.

Kleha believed that part of a marketer's role was to embody the customer in every meeting, telling them that when you point out what the customer would think about something or what the user would do in reaction to a certain decision, it becomes a much different conversation that other people can't challenge. And if you back that up with quotes from customers about the company or data that helps support how customers use various things, it could play a powerful role in the decision making.

They were floored. Not only was Kleha qualified on paper, but she was also a treasure trove of insights, brave enough to challenge the status quo, and driven by the purest of intentions—all things Figma held in high regard. To their surprise (and relief), she accepted the role of Figma's Chief Customer Officer, enthused by the prospect of getting to think holistically across the whole revenue picture and the full customer journey.

She applied her hard-won lessons to her new position and became a trusted voice among employees and leadership around such issues as when freemium made sense in SaaS, the right time to add sales or customer success to a self-service business, and the implications of product-led growth (PLG) on culture. She simplified Figma's go-to-market model through a combination of self-service and sales-assisted motions, helped establish two additional pricing tiers, oversaw the building of an enterprise sales team, and balanced the gender ratio among their team, which soon saw more females than males in leadership positions. She also fostered Figma's relationships with its customers (and theirs to each other) through new Figma Community initiatives, among them an annual design conference and an online publication for design systems creators, designers, developers, and managers to share lessons and stories.

Four years after Kleha joined Figma, its annual revenue had grown 2,600% to $81.1 million. Its customer base grew by three million users, many of whom were companies like Dropbox, Rakuten, Slack, Twitter, and Volvo. Its employee count nearly doubled in size, as had its product offerings. In 2022, Figma was acquired by Adobe for $20 billion.[17]

Dig Wider, Not Deeper

We know full well that business success (or failure, for that matter) does not rest on the shoulders of one or two people. For every business out there, many factors determine whether a venture will take off: having a solid concept, being thorough in its implementation, anticipating market fluctuation, and marketing it properly to clients. But the importance of having the right people on your team is foundational. It starts by recognizing that importance and then taking an intentional look at what "the right people" actually means.

Many of our clients are venture capitalists looking to invest in the next big thing. When funding new start-ups, investors have a common objective: build out a stellar founding team that can ensure the success of their investment. They want to see people who can take a crazy ambitious idea and run with it. They think big and want to see companies that are outliers. For a business to be an outlier, it stands to reason that something about the team will be too. It probably looks dissimilar from other investments—not in every way, but in some ways. That's a critical part of a company, and it pops out in the individuals on the team too. Not everyone fits the mold, or checks all the boxes, or has every requirement perfectly articulated on their résumé. (And how is it that we're still using résumés? In 2022, the résumé doesn't look much different from how it did in 1952.)

For endeavors like this, we've found our clients like to go about recruitment unconventionally. Typically this means that frontrunners with the desired qualifications get moved to the top of the queue while exciting contenders can easily be disregarded as "not what we're looking for." Recruiters talk about medalists (Gold, Silver, etc.). It's an easy metaphor to overlay onto team building, but it misses some fundamentals. Many forward-thinking venture capitalists believe that potential trumps pedigree, and choose a metaphor from math instead of sports. They say to hire for "slope over intercept." After all, if you want to innovate, you need to solve for that ability first, and it's hard to fit into a school degree or level ranking.

Many innovative companies will often want to find a failed founder; they want to know the candidate tried something that didn't work because it's guaranteed they learned invaluable lessons from it. It's a clear way to filter for someone who is guaranteed to be ambitious. Others want someone who founded something that was then acquired for tens of millions; the candidate was able to build something impressive enough to be sold. It's a way to find people who can execute against something ambitious enough, and work through enough ambiguity, to build something meaningful.

Some companies will look for a work history that shows someone hasn't stayed anywhere beyond a year or two; the candidate seems to always be looking for the next thing. It can be frowned upon as job-hopping, or it can also be more positive, showing an appetite for risk, or knowing how to pivot and take in new data and business knowledge to their next stop. Others look for a technical candidate who didn't attend a top computer science school like Stanford, MIT, Berkeley, or Harvard; they want to see that someone has worked in the field relying on their know-how versus university clout.

Some search for people who attended historically black colleges and universities (HBCUs) as a way to foster diversity on their team. These candidates typically get one-tenth the outreach of those who are sourced based on their proximity to historically black communities. Others search for a candidate who's a first-generation college student; the potential hire will likely bring a level of pride, vigilance, and determination into whatever they do.

Some seek former athletes who played college sports; those candidates know how to persevere and are resilient enough to bounce back from failure. They know how to work hard on something for a long time and achieve at an elite level. They understand winning, losing, rallying when things get tough, and picking up their teammates. Others seek people with unusual backgrounds, such as someone who's been a longtime volunteer for sea turtle conservation or has a history of being a novice monk (seriously); a candidate who seeks the road less traveled is inclined to be audacious, inspired, and adaptable.

Some look for veterans; candidates with military experience are known to be punctual, versatile, and have a work ethic that won't quit. Others look for candidates who took a sabbatical; it's seen as a positive when they worked really hard, found enough success that they wanted to pull back and think things over, then build more intrinsic motivation and conviction for their next move.

While standard recruitment tools don't always allow for such niche discoveries, we built our platform under the assumption that everything about a person feeds into how we think about their fit for a job. The intangibles matter, and when possible, we make them actionable. And while the majority of our clients prefer a more straightforward approach to sourcing, rethinking the prerequisites for a successful hire is the type of out-of-the-box thinking we value. Exploring alternative new-hire criteria in no way negates our respect for companies looking for graduates from top universities who've worked at reputable companies; it merely promotes the idea that when looking for a diamond in the rough, you need to look somewhere other than a jewelry store.

Reading Between the Lines

There's no wrong or right way to filter and assess potential candidates; it's all about determining what's truly most important to the job. Sometimes the perfect pedigree and high-profile experience is exactly what the role needs. Other times, even the most well-crafted job description may not capture every person who might flourish in the position.

When a family-owned electronics retailer wanted to find a new CEO to professionalize its management and expand its operations, the outgoing chief executive and the board pinpointed the relevant competencies for the job. They handed it over to a recruiter who sourced suitable candidates, and the man they hired had all the right credentials: he attended top schools, had experience working for credible organizations in the industry, and was currently a successful country manager for an admired company. Even more important, he'd scored above the target level for each of the competencies they'd identified. But none of that mattered. Despite the impressive background and apparent great fit, the new hire could not adjust to the massive technological, economical, and regulatory changes occurring in the market at the time. He was asked to leave after three years of lackluster performance.

In contrast, that same recruiter was asked to source a project manager role at a small brewery, Quinsa, that dominated the beer market in the southern region of Latin America. He was having a hard time identifying a large enough pool of people with the right industry and background outlined by the employer, so he threw caution to the wind and contacted business executive and economist Pedro Algorta, a fellow student he'd known from his college days, about the position. A survivor of the infamous 1972 plane crash in the Andes, famously documented in the book and movie *Alive*, Algorta was certainly an intriguing choice. Well, except for three small details: He had no experience in consumer goods, was unfamiliar with the province in Argentina where the brewery was located, and had never worked in sales or marketing, both key areas of expertise.

But the recruiter couldn't get past Algorta's potential; he was motivated, curious, insightful, engaged, and determined. He felt Algorta could succeed at the brewing company because he had all those qualities, not because he possessed a specific skill set or competencies. And those qualities were clearly demonstrated during his harrowing ordeal in the Andes. He proved his motivation by playing a critical yet humble role—providing sustenance for the explorers who eventually saved the rest of the group. He melted snow for them to drink and removed small pieces of flesh from the dead bodies of fellow victims to serve as food. Instead of surrendering to despair, Algorta got curious about the environment that surrounded him, noticing water coming off the ice. He saw that it flowed east, leading him—and only him—to the insight that the dying pilot had misreported their position: they were on the Argentine side of the mountain range, not the Chilean side. His engagement and determination were also on display over those 72 days. He dependably tended to his dying friend who had suffered numerous leg fractures, trying to distract the young man from his painful reality. He encouraged his fellow survivors to maintain hope and persuaded them all to condone the consumption of their own bodies, should they die, describing it as "an act of love."[18]

Ultimately, Quinsa heeded the instincts of the recruiter and hired Algorta. The decision proved to be a smart one. Algorta was quickly promoted to general manager of the brewery and then CEO of Quinsa's flagship Quilmes brewery. He became a vital member of the team that transformed Quinsa from a family-owned enterprise to a booming, respected conglomerate with a management team considered at the time to be among the best in Latin America.[19]

Although Algorta's tenure pales in comparison to the trials he experienced in the Andes, the same characteristics served him in his career at Quinsa. For one, he showed amazing determination. When the construction of a new brewery he'd been hired to lead ran out of funds just as he took over, quitting wasn't an option; instead, he pushed to get the necessary financing. And when Argentina was shaken by hyperinflation and devaluation a few months later, he pressed on and the facility was up and running in 15 months. He was also a curious executive, always going out of his way to meet customers, clients, and workers across all levels, listening to the voices that usually either went unheard or were disregarded. As a result, he accepted and supported some truly innovative marketing initiatives, allowing Quilmes to multiply its sales eightfold and achieve record profitability. He displayed great intuition in his hiring decisions—the future CEOs of both Nestlé and Quilmes were among his most notable hires—and in his strategic ones: for example, he made a bold move to divest all noncore assets so that the company could use the proceeds to expand the regional brewery business. His engagement transformed an inefficient and even vicious culture at Quilmes; his insistence that bosses and subordinates come together in open meetings set a precedent that was later implemented throughout the company. Perhaps the best example of the purity of his motives came at the end of his 10-year stint at the company, when, for sound strategic reasons, he recommended that it abandon the agribusiness project he was leading, essentially voting himself out of a job.

In the midst of vetting candidates, recruiters can fail to notice one crucial thing: potential. And in an industry where they spend an average of only 7.4 seconds skimming a résumé, it can be an easy thing to miss.[20] With contributing factors like a large candidate pool and pressure to quickly fill a role, many recruiters are left with nominal insight into the talent sitting before them; hidden in plain sight may be the very qualifications that would make the applicant an ideal contender.

We can learn a lot from Quilmes and Quibi. The team makes the company. And when the fit is exactly right, amazing things happen. But that's the hard part: the right fit.

2 | Diverse Intangibles

We've all heard the myth: The entrepreneurial giants of the world had to fight their way to the top, single-handedly and against all odds. And of course, that's the story we're told. Myths are engaging—we love heroes—and the tale of one person's trajectory is much easier to understand than that of a group. As individuals, we make sense of the world through stories. And stories about other individuals feel relatable. We can see some of ourselves in our heroes, and we like it. These stories fuel our imaginations in ways that feel empowering and encouraging, and are far more engaging than an exploration of a team's dynamic.

But success stories about the lone hero are misleading. When we're faced with pressure or complexity, it's often the specific actions and skills of many, as opposed to those of one person, that make a complex endeavor successful. We see it time and again, in sports, politics, communities, family life, and of course, business.

That doesn't negate the importance of that "one person" though—for it's a bunch of individuals who make up a team, and the uniqueness each person brings to the table determines the team's overall cohesiveness, productivity, and success. Individual parts add up to the whole, and individuality matters. Our uniqueness matters.

Notice we said uniqueness, not talent. Contrary to popular belief, building a team with lots of really talented people doesn't necessarily guarantee a team's success. Research shows that groups of problem solvers with diverse viewpoints can outperform groups of high-ability problem solvers. The types of skills that come from different points of view doesn't just beat raw talent, insofar as it is more talent. It is something else altogether. A study published in *Psychological Science* looked at the relative merit of having a team made up of the very best problem solvers versus a team whose members were accomplished problem solvers but had a diverse set of approaches for tackling those problems. The results showed that the diverse teams outperformed the teams made up of the very best individuals.

In today's work environment, diversity, equity, and inclusion (DEI) is a top business priority. Finding and hiring underrepresented candidates ensures companies avoid groupthink and consider new approaches in order to remain competitive. But we'll go one further. Done well, DEI actively recognizes that these diverse backgrounds, worldviews, ideas, perspectives, and cultural lenses are what influence innovation, efficiency, employee retention, and, yes, revenue. The different perspectives and points of view fill in the gaps that solving for these core principles "on paper" can never do. The emphasis therefore shifts from the obvious type of diversity that you can see to the type of diversity you can't.

Just ask Shane Battier.

In 2010, the Miami Heat tried to build a dream team by signing Lebron James, Dwayne Wade, and Chris Bosh. The trio, who became known as the Big Three, promised fans they would win many championships, but they struggled to even win close games in the regular season. They lost the 2011 NBA finals to a Dallas Mavericks team that was, by most measures, less talented. So the next year, instead of picking up another star, they picked up Shane Battier.

Fans were not impressed. Over the course of his decade-long career playing for the Memphis Grizzlies and the Houston Rockets,

Battier only averaged 9.6 points and 4.7 rebounds per game.[1] He was criticized in the media for his lack of athleticism and all the limitations that stemmed from it: he didn't run pick-and-roll, couldn't dribble, wasn't fast enough, and didn't dish out many assists.

In a sport where a team scores on average about 100 points a game, two out of three NBA games are decided by fewer than six points—two or three possessions. That small margin of error significantly raises the importance of every little thing that happens on the court, and by extension, *who* is on the court. A natural inclination would be to fill your team with high scorers, which the Heat did. In the 2010–2011 season, James averaged 26.7 points per game, followed closely by Wade with 25.5 points and Bosh with 18.7.[2] But despite making it to the NBA Finals that year, they failed to go home with a ring.

Over his 10 seasons in the league, Shane Battier had only averaged double-digit points three times, and consistently ranked among the bottom in rebounds, steals, blocks, and assists. Heading into the 2011–2012 season, he had never even come close to winning a championship ring. But ironically, he was the one player Miami president Pat Riley called in free agency to push the Heat over the top. He wanted to build on something he saw with the Houston Rockets.

Back in 2007 when Daryl Morey was appointed the new general manager for the Rockets, he was charged with turning around the losing team. The problem? A huge chunk of the team's allotted payroll was already committed to two superstars, Tracy McGrady and Yao Ming, which meant Morey had to find ways to improve the Rockets without spending money. So he scoured the league looking for non-superstars that he thought were undervalued. Someone who was impactful and effective, just maybe not traditionally talented. On his list of 15, close to the top, was the Memphis Grizzlies' forward Shane Battier.

Morey's career did not start in sports management, but at the MITRE Corporation as a computer scientist. He studied computer science and statistics at Northwestern, and built advanced analysis systems for the intelligence community at MITRE. He learned about the power of data, and how it could be used to influence decision making in complex, uncertain environments, with lots at stake. Intelligence problems are rarely simple; they require working on the data with absolute rigor. But they also require analysts to keep asking why and live in the data until things make sense.

Morey's technology background was perfect for sports. He left to join EY Parthenon as a consultant specializing in advising sports leaders on strategy, and then STATS Inc, which developed the software featured in *Moneyball*. It is Morey's different point of view that set him apart from other general managers in the NBA. He leaned on a mix of data and basketball to make decisions about what would make the most impact to the team.

In reviewing the data, Morey noticed Battier wasn't grabbing huge numbers of rebounds, but he had an uncanny ability to improve his teammates' rebounding. He didn't shoot much, but when he did, he took only the most efficient shots and had a knack for getting to teammates who were in a position to do the same. On defense, although he routinely guarded the NBA's most prolific scorers, he significantly reduced their shooting percentages. But here is what Morey really noticed: despite the obvious weaknesses Battier's game had, when he was on the court, every one of his teams was statistically more likely to win. Morey could see how the minute-by-minute action of the game tied to outcomes by using data that others couldn't easily see. He did another type of analysis. He saw the outcome of Battier's performance, and kept digging to get the right data that explained why. Morey knew how to look for it, because that was core to his skill set. His worldview was a mix of GM, analyst, statistician, and technologist.

Before the Rockets traded for Battier, the front-office analysts studied his value. They knew all sorts of details about his efficiency and his ability to reduce the efficiency of his opponents. They knew, for example, that stars guarded by Battier suddenly lost their shooting touch. What they didn't know was why.

It turned out that Battier was like Morey in his approach: He studied the data on the superstars he was usually assigned to guard, determined their strengths and weaknesses, and then tried to defend in such a way that combated what they were good at and capitalized on what they weren't. For example, the numbers showed him that Allen Iverson was one of the most efficient scorers in the NBA when he went to his right, but when he went to his left, he killed his team. The Golden State Warriors forward Stephen Jackson was statistically better going to his right, but he loved to go to his left, and went almost twice as often. Battier soaked in information like that, and knowing the odds, he pursued an inherently uncertain strategy with total certainty.

Upon being traded to the Rockets, Battier was given a special package of information before every game. The only player to receive it, he sifted through highly statistical data which essentially broke down the floor into many discrete zones and calculated the odds of opponents making shots from various places on the court, under contrasting degrees of defensive pressure, and in different relationships to other players. This was the very information he reviewed prior to the Rockets' game against the Lakers.

Kobe Bryant seemingly had no weaknesses to his game, but Battier noticed that there were places on the court, and starting points for his shot, that rendered him less likely to help his team. He noticed that when Bryant drove to the basket, he was exactly as likely to go to his left as to his right, but when he went to his left, he was less effective. When he shot directly after receiving a pass, he was more efficient than when he shot after dribbling. He was deadly if he got into the lane and also if he got to the baseline; between the two, less so. With Battier armed with his intel, the Rockets insisted he guard Bryant. And what happened was remarkable.

When Bryant was in the game and Battier was on him, the Lakers' offense was worse than if the NBA's best player had taken the night off. Bryant missed more shots than he made. His view of the basket was consistently blocked by Battier's hand. At one point after not getting a call, Bryant screamed at the referees, hurled the ball, and was whistled for a technical foul. Battier not only guarded one of the greatest and smartest offensive threats ever to play the game, but he also rendered him a detriment to his own team.

Battier was an invaluable part of the team because he contributed things that no other player did. The Rockets didn't just want to beef up their defense—they wanted a player who brought something different to their defensive strategy. While there were plenty of talented defensive players they could have recruited, Battier relied more on his knowledge of the game and his opponent, rather than his athleticism to become a stopper. Battier excelled in everything that could be acquired through intellect, instead of relying on innate ability. The Rockets were one of the first NBA teams to embrace the sort of statistical analysis now universal in the league. Morey and Battier joined forces to build a way of operating, from the data to the court, that proved successful. It was a unique team perspective, embodied by two unique people, in Battier and Morey. And that uniqueness was exactly what the Heat needed.

In Battier's first two seasons with Miami, they won back-to-back championships. His data-based insights on his opponents was a key part of their strategy, and his versatile and disruptive play as a result of those insights was the type of contribution the team needed to succeed. He also spread his wealth of knowledge by giving his teammates meaningful information at crucial times. Before a big game against the Oklahoma City Thunder, Battier told Lebron James, "Hey, when you guard Kevin Durant, make him shoot over his left shoulder." It worked. After that, James would say, "Hey Batman, what you got on this guy?"[3]

Morey went on to found the MIT Sloan Sports Analytics Conference, a must-attend for back-office sports executives. He's routinely recognized as one of the most progressive thinkers in sports, especially when it comes to analytical methods. Morey was the NBA's Executive of the Year in 2018 and now runs operations for the Philadelphia 76ers.

The five players on a basketball team are far more than the sum of their parts, as is the case with any type of team. But people can misinterpret teamwork as something related to the efforts made by a team when, in reality, teamwork combines the individual efforts of each team member to achieve a common goal. And it's the specific contributions of those individuals that give the team its edge.

The Big Picture

Of course, teams aren't just about sports; often they need to solve a problem, and team members contribute certain skills to provide the best chance at finding a solution. Other times, it's not packaged as a problem but as a goal, and they work together to bring it to fruition. Regardless, the essence of a team is shared commitment. Without it, groups perform as individuals; with it, they become a powerful unit of collective performance.

In 1969, NASA's Neil Armstrong and Buzz Aldrin became the first men to walk on the moon. While they've gone down in history for the momentous achievement, they wouldn't have made it off the ground without the support of a massive team. Over 300,000 men and women collaborated on the Apollo 11 launch, from surveyors to engineers to geologists to the astronauts themselves, and all understood the goal they were working towards. In fact, when President Kennedy visited NASA in 1962 and asked a janitor what he did, he proudly replied, "I'm helping to put a man on the moon."[4]

Many people would think this is just a cute story—that it may have felt good for people on the ground to believe they were instrumental in putting the first human on the moon even though it was clearly the work of just a few people that had created the most impact. However, just a year later, the public got to see just how important that team of diverse minds on the ground was.

As the Apollo 13 shuttle approached the moon, an oxygen tank exploded. No longer was their mission to complete another moonwalk. Instead, they scrambled to conserve energy while also frantically trying to lower the carbon dioxide levels onboard. Don Arabian was one of the experts who would be consulted in such an emergency. He ran the Mission Evaluation Room engineering team and was known to be a brilliant engineer with a loud, booming voice. But there was an interesting thing about Don that would prove to be crucial in the mission to save the astronauts.

Despite his fierce and assertive personality, Don was known for something unique. According to Jerry Woodfill, who designed the very systems that were now screaming alerts at the team, Don "feared no man above or below his paygrade . . . he was fair with lower level workers and respected their knowledge."[5]

So when the team ran into a problem, Don did what he did best—he asked questions and worked alongside his colleagues to unlock the knowledge that he lacked. The team gathered their supplies, and because whatever solution they concocted needed to be replicated by the astronauts, supplies were limited to only the odds and ends that would be onboard the space shuttle: plastic bags, hoses, socks, and duct tape. Then they got to work.

The astronauts had racked up hundreds of hours in space over many missions. They had impressive degrees and had graduated from prestigious military academies. The team members supporting them from the ground all had their own specialties. The most senior member of the Manned Spacecraft Center had even created the standard operating procedure for flights, yet found himself in a scenario where absolutely nothing was standard.

It was an exercise they could never have prepared for. Little by little, the team's solution evolved. Soon, they had crafted a filter that would eliminate the carbon dioxide that was creeping up on the team. When the hoses collapsed, the team ripped apart a cardboard logbook to fashion some supports. They sealed the leaks with duct tape and ran it through the simulators. It worked!

Next they were tasked with communicating the design to the astronauts. Unable to send a photo 200,000 miles into space, they carefully dictated the 19 steps needed to build the CO_2 scrubber they now referred to as "the mailbox." The astronauts successfully built the contraption and saw the carbon dioxide levels start to drop immediately. The shuttle returned home and, after a few tense moments that caught the riveted public holding their breath, the men climbed out of the pod to wild cheers and celebration, weary but otherwise unharmed.

The team that had sprung into action was full of specialized, talented people who had devoted their lives to solving problems in a narrow scope. But Apollo 13 flight director Gene Kranz knew they didn't have time to methodically consult each department. Instead, they'd need to put their heads together and move quickly. Hundreds of people worked tirelessly for almost 90 hours straight, giving crash courses in the pieces they understood and learning from the brilliant minds that specialized in something else.

These heroes in Mission Control didn't have experience in space. But they each brought unique skills to the table. One was a Life Scout in the Boy Scouts of America. Another was a medical doctor. One had been rejected as an astronaut but had extensive experience as an airplane pilot. All of them had something to contribute that helped make the mission successful. The team was built to carry out the precisely mapped out mission. They had the skills, but their shared commitment to the mission made the team work. Everyone had a duty that used their individual skill sets to complete a regimented plan. But when things went awry, the astronauts were saved because of the team's ability to think creatively and work collaboratively. The mission pushed them to think as a single, functioning unit, not as individuals focused on their narrow set of tasks. They focused on the outcome, and what they could do together. As Kranz said, "I don't care what anything was *designed* to do. I care about what it *can* do."[6] The team was designed to be a steady force. But it was actually capable of doing much more.

There are endless examples of effective teamwork and the groundbreaking impact it can have on outcomes. And especially among today's lightning-fast, idea-oriented organizations, the emphasis on team collaboration has never been more important. It's why investors in start-ups often value the quality of the team and the interaction between the founding members more than the idea itself. It's why 90% of investors think the quality of the management team is the single most important nonfinancial factor when evaluating an IPO. And that's why, when their top team is working together toward a shared vision, a company is 1.9 times more likely to achieve above-median financial performance.[7]

Building an effective team can be a hard thing to get right, and organizations often undergo massive restructuring as a way to course correct. Some examples: In 2014, the new CEO of Microsoft, Satya Nadella, cut 14% of the staff in order to "eliminate its destructive internal competition"; in 2018, Hulu eliminated key management positions, hired a new Chief Technology Officer (CTO) and Chief Data Officer (CDO), and added 200 tech and product employees; Tesla laid off about 9% of its employees, accounting for more than 3,000 job cuts, and "flattened the management structure" as a way to improve communication and efficiency of its operations; Invision, a design and productivity technology company, changed its product strategy over an 18-month period, and to do so, it replaced the entire executive team, completely transforming the culture of the organization in the process.[8]

Employee turnover is an inevitable aspect of business. On average, a company will experience 18% turnover of its workforce every year; 6% is involuntary, meaning loss of staff due to a reduction in force or termination due to poor performance, while 12% leave on their own volition. Regardless, the cost of turnover is significant. In 2019 alone, it cost US industries more than $630 billion.[9]

The financial impact on an organization is not the only consequence; turnover has costs that don't appear on a financial report. For example, reduction in employee morale and engagement, increased burnout, and the loss of organizational knowledge when a key employee leaves can suddenly threaten to disrupt the health and wellness of employees and companies alike. There is a compounding negative value to making the wrong hires. It puts into focus the importance of recruiting the right people who will add distinct value to the team—the first time around.

This can be challenging, of course. There is a lot to consider when building a team, not least of which is combating the antithesis of distinct value: hiring people who are just like you. Research by the Kellogg School of Management on the unconscious bias of modern professional services firms found that employers were looking to hire people who were not just competent but who were culturally similar to themselves in relation to leisure pursuits, experience, and self-presentation style.[10]

Few question the cultural fit paradigm, although there is a rising tide of objectors to cultural fit hiring who say it leads to homogeneous teams that lack diversity in nature and outlook, as well as the flexibility, innovation, and scope to react to a diverse and dynamic environment.

While consistency can make a very predictable culture, diversity is strength. Just think of it in the context of soft skills: you need detailed, analytical, conservative fiscal types as much as you need energetic, outgoing "let's tackle the world" salespeople; you need people who communicate ideas effectively to others, both orally and in writing, and you need people who can communicate through pictures, images, colors, and movement; you need dreamers and you need "get it done" implementers. A team that's heavy on certain dispositions will fall short in the areas that are underrepresented, and that same methodology applies to the more in-depth diversification of a team.

The Case for Diversity

Diversity has become something of a buzzword. However, organizations that simply look at diversity as a trend are missing out on the depth and value that truly diverse and inclusive organizations bring.

While the word itself denotes racial and social justice issues, those are just facets of a larger conversation. Diversity means variety, and extends to such lengths as its name implies: a broad variety of racial, ethnic, socioeconomic, and cultural backgrounds and various life-styles, skill sets, experience, and interests. When teams are filled with a variety of people—that is, they each have something unique to offer rather than more of the same—they bring a well-roundedness that sets the team up to see, think, and do things in ways the individuals wouldn't normally on their own.

Numerous studies have shown that diversity, both inherent (e.g., race and gender) and acquired (e.g., experience and cultural back-ground), is associated with business success. A recent report on 366 public companies found that those in the top quartile for ethnic and racial diversity were 35% more likely to have financial returns above their industry mean, and those in the top quartile for gender diversity were 21% more likely to have returns above the industry mean.[11] Financial success aside, diversity creates better working conditions for everyone. When comparing the FAANG company with the most and least racial diversity, the company with the most has current employ-ees that stayed an average of 25% longer than the company with the least.

Another report shows that diverse personal experiences, such as living or working abroad, are associated with greater creativity. Inter-estingly, bicultural individuals display more creativity, deeper infor-mation processing, and greater perspective taking.[12] These distinctive strengths lend themselves to distinct thinking styles, and research has shown that a group with cognitive diversity will perform better at problem solving than a group with higher intelligence but a uniform cognitive style.

We think this mentality speaks to the powerful value of cross-functional teams. While most departments are organized by expertise and purpose, companies often build teams with people from various departments so the members' unique skills, experience, and knowl-edge can form a melting pot of ideas, approaches, and vantage points. These teams have a broader range of abilities that extend to the intan-gibles, the root of their thinking, the origin of their abilities. There are many examples of inspiring, massively productive groups of diverse teams achieving fantastic goals.

Northwestern Mutual Life, a financial services mutual organization, has long embraced this cross-functional approach. In the 1950s, the company put together its first cross-functional team by drawing people from disparate departments to study the impact that computers would have on the financial industry. This helped Northwestern develop one of the country's first information systems departments, which translated into a huge competitive advantage in an increasingly computer-driven market. Today, the company still relies on cross-functional teams, though have fine-tuned the concept by appointing one person to each of their teams who is not a stakeholder at all. They believe outsiders, because they're not locked into a customary way of thinking, bring a necessary and fresh perspective to an issue.

CarMax, the largest seller of used cars in the United States, leans heavily upon cross-functional teams to drive customer-centric innovation. But the cross-functional philosophy doesn't just apply to teams that are focused on the company's products. Many CarMax store locations are classified as "cross-functional stores," in which employees are expected to have a holistic understanding of the business. Associates are trained to perform multiple functions, with high-potential employees receiving "fast-track" development to prepare them to manage a cross-functional workplace.

One of our clients, Scoop Technologies, is a platform that helps optimize hybrid work environments. During its early days, cofounder and Chief Product Officer Jonathan Sadow oversaw the siloed marketing, operations, and analytics teams. He realized he was actually leading a collection of functions that all had to do with one goal: growth. He changed his title to Chief Growth Officer and merged the fragmented teams into one division, unifying their respective specialties around a common goal. It's no wonder he was personally responsible for half of the 13,000 candidates Scoop sourced. He had an overarching view; he understood what the team needed and how candidates could contribute cross-functionally.

Diversity is a cornerstone of cross-functional teams, but it isn't confined to diversity of expertise. The more diverse the group is, the more effective and productive it will be at meeting its goals; this means variances of age, status, background, disposition, gender, race, and tenure with the organization. These inclusions not only allow employers to widen the candidate pool, but ensure they're able to build a team filled with people who are inherently different from one another.

In Good Company

If you define innovation as a company's ability to creatively adapt to its business circumstances, you quickly conclude that diversity and inclusion are essential to business success. A diversified team can ensure a broader range of perspectives, leading to a wider range of information and a more balanced outcome. When it comes to racial or ethnic diversity, specifically, it tends to improve the performance of decision-making groups.

A study published in the *Journal of Personality and Social Psychology* examined racial composition and group decision making in a mock jury scenario. Researchers found that juries that included white and Black members led to more detailed deliberations and fairer verdicts. Further results showed that placing white jurors in diverse groups raised their performance level, encouraging them to cite more facts, make fewer mistakes, deliberate longer, and conduct broader and more accurate discussions—compared to peers in all-white mock juries. Racially mixed juries were also much more willing to discuss issues of racism.[13]

Prioritizing racial diversity allows companies to adopt different lenses to solve challenges, operate the organization, and ensure its sustainability. When Ursula Burns was named CEO of Xerox in 2009, she was the first Black female CEO to ever head a Fortune 500 company. Even though she had been at Xerox since the early 1980s, she admitted she didn't know nearly half of what she needed to know to run the company. But she had an intense work ethic and was used to thriving in a corporate setting as an outsider—being both Black and female.

Raised by a single Panamanian immigrant mother in a New York City housing project, Burns came "face-to-face with racism and sexism almost every day" while growing up and was told in school that though she was smart, she had three things going against her: she was Black, poor, and a girl. These significant experiences gave her the gift of grit, later saying, "White women discard you. Black men discard you. White men don't even know you're there. So you have to have grit and keep pushing, keep pushing, keep pushing."[14]

And she did. Working her way up Xerox's corporate ladder, she became its CEO at the height of the Great Recession. She and her team led the struggling company through the acquisition of Affiliated Computer Services (ACS), the world's largest diversified business process outsourcing firm, and oversaw Xerox's subsequent formation into two independent companies: Xerox Corporation and Conduent Incorporated. During her tenure, Xerox increased revenue by $5 billion and was named one of the "20 Most Responsible US Companies," "World's Most Ethical Companies," "World's Most Reputable Companies," and "Top 100 Most Diverse & Inclusive Companies."[15] When people doubted if Xerox could transform itself from the business machines company that had defined photocopying for decades into a provider in the newer, lucrative world of business services, Burns wasn't phased—she had been doubted her entire life.

The uniqueness of Ursula Burns wasn't simply that she was Black or female; it was the formative experiences she had had and the subsequent perspectives she gained as a result of being Black and female. And that mindset is what separates the progressive companies from the revolutionary ones.

Sodexo, an international hospitality company, has a mantra among its hiring staff: "Gender balance is our business." Women currently account for 55% of its more than 400,000-person staff and make up 58% of their board. Sodexo's commitment to achieving optimal gender balance has increased employee engagement by 4%, gross profits by 23%, and brand image by 5%.[16]

Marriott, the international hotel chain, was one of the earliest adopters of diversity and inclusion initiatives. Of its 7,500-plus hotels, more than 1,500 are owned by women and diverse partners, and women-owned business enterprises make up approximately 10% of its supply chain. LGBTQ+ inclusion is also a top priority for the hotel giant. For over a decade, Marriott has earned and sustained a perfect score on the Human Rights Campaign's Corporate Equality Index (CEI) based on their longstanding support of policies for LGBTQ+ associates including health insurance benefits for transgender care and gender affirmation care.[16,17]

Intel, one of the largest computer hardware and software companies in the world, established IGLOBE (Intel Gay, Lesbian, Bisexual, or Transgender Employees) as an employee research group back in 1994. Today, IGLOBE has 13 chapters globally and actively drives awareness of issues impacting the LGBTQ+ community, serves as a support network for its members, and offers a mentorship program where experienced Intel workers can mentor new workers who are also members of the LGBTQ+ community.[18]

SAP, a multinational software company, has an "Autism at Work" program that employs more than 180 autistic workers, and a partnership with Historically Black Colleges and Universities (HBCUs) called Project Propel in which SAP teaches its software to undergraduates and MBA students with the goal of building a pipeline of potential new hires.[19]

Leidos, an American engineering company, focuses on "neurodiversity" by hiring employees with special needs, ranging from autism to dyspraxia to social anxiety disorders. Leidos sees the potential of people with these disorders; research shows that some conditions can result in higher-than-average abilities when it comes to things like pattern recognition, memory, or mathematics.

Abbott, the medical device company headquartered in Chicago, focuses on hiring veterans and providing mentorship opportunities in the form of structured, yearlong developmental partnerships. Its career page includes a "military skills translator" that allows veterans to search for open positions using military codes.

Headspace, a client of ours in the mindfulness and meditation space, utilizes a more comprehensive approach to diverse hiring. One of their initiatives includes pre-identifying the role, the team, and the function they're hiring for and then cross-referencing that with data and metrics regarding the underrepresented groups in that space to create a level of intentionality around the search.

For certain companies we've worked with, fostering diversity in the workplace means filling quotas or creating HR policies. But that's not what it's about. Hiring for diversity means creating a team made of people as varied as the world we live in. It includes the tangible, visible differences in each of us, such as race, gender, and age, and expands to intangible or invisible qualities, including diversity of thought or opinion, sexual orientation, or even something like dyslexia or attention deficit disorder. Many times the tangible informs the intangible, as was the case with Ursula Burns, while other times it requires deliberate curiosity and observation to uncover the strengths hidden below the surface, as with Shane Battier. Either route leads to the same reality: everyone has something that makes them different, and the aggregation of that uniqueness is what successful teams are built around.

Intangibles in Action

In the 85th minute of the qualifying match for the 2011 Women's World Cup, the United States and Italy were tied 0–0. American soccer fans were understandably anxious, but that anxiety reached new heights as they watched newcomer Alex Morgan get subbed in. It wasn't her newness that worried fans, per se; rather, they were more puzzled by the reasoning. The United States women's national soccer team (USWNT) roster that year had no shortage of famous names with proven track records: Abby Wambach, Carli Lloyd, and Megan Rapinoe. What could Alex Morgan do that those players couldn't?

The world soon found out.

Midfielder Carli Lloyd kicked a long ball forward and it was subtly flicked by Wambach right into the path of a running Morgan, who slotted the ball into the far post just out of reach of the Italian goalkeeper. Alex Morgan, the 21-year-old who had never played on a stage this big, who had sat on the sidelines for the entirety of the game up to that point, and who was flanked by some of the best female soccer players in the world, was the one who scored the winning goal that would take the United States to the World Cup.

Was it her speed? Her strong left foot? Was she just a rookie with something to prove? Was it a lucky break?

An argument could be made for all of these. But the real reason she came in clutch was the result of her intangibles: she was fearless, adaptable, and decisive.

When Alex was six years old, she ran back and forth along the sidelines during her older sister's soccer games. She actually had two older sisters, which meant twice the amount of ground to cover, twice the number of games per week, and twice the level of embarrassment felt by her sisters. Alex wasn't trying to be the annoying younger sister; she was just doing what she'd always done: trying to keep up.

Regardless, after an impressive amount of cumulative miles run and soccer games watched, Alex announced to her mom, "I want to do that. I want to *be that*."

So once Alex was a little older, her mom signed her up to play. Shortly thereafter, Alex set her sights on something bigger than emulating her sisters and told her mom, "I want to be a professional soccer player."

That would likely be a problem. This was circa 1997 and there was no such thing as a professional women's soccer player, at least not really. The highest ambition for females was to play soccer in the Olympics, which had only been introduced as an official sport of the Olympic games in 1996. The second-best thing was to play at the college level, and even that was a relatively recent development

following the passing of Title IX, which outlawed gender-based discrimination for federally funded education programs. The third
option was the national interregional soccer league for women (later
called the W-League), the newly launched semiprofessional, open
league that gave college players the opportunity to play against international players while maintaining their college eligibility.

Suffice it to say, there was no clear path, no real room for growth,
little-to-no compensation, and not much hope for an actual career. It
would be Alex's first—but not last—encounter with the glass ceiling.

Despite all signs pointing to the dire fate of her daughter's dream,
Alex's mom told her, "Great, let's make that happen."

Those words may sound surprising (read: irresponsible, unrealis-
tic) to some, but not if you knew Alex's mom. As a married mother
of three daughters, she did it all: worked full-time, took her girls to
endless soccer, gymnastics, and softball practices, cooked dinner every
night, all while attending night school for five years to get her MBA.
She wasn't signaling to her daughters that they must run themselves
ragged to survive life; she was showing them how to dauntlessly work
hard to achieve whatever they deemed important.

So that's what Alex did. And at age 13, when her soccer coach
told her she wasn't good enough to be on the team and would be
relegated to the practice squad, she naturally felt defeated. But not for
long. Maybe she didn't appear refined enough, but she knew she
wanted it more than anybody and she was determined to show the
coach why she belonged. Getting knocked down only mattered if
you didn't get back up.

As Alex grew up, she played basketball, softball, volleyball, soccer,
and ran track. This range of sports provided her with adaptability, but
not the kind you'd expect. Yes, playing different sports requires different types of physicality, incorporates different equipment and rules,
and promotes different mindsets (team versus individual sport, for
example). It makes for a well-rounded athlete, and that was certainly
true in Alex's case. But her real adaptability came once she dedicated
herself solely to soccer.

Youth athletes who want to embrace soccer as a year-round sport play club soccer (interchangeably called competitive soccer or travel soccer). Alex played on four different teams per year, which meant that every couple of months, she had a new coach, new teammates, and new plays and strategies to master. Four times every year, she needed to refind her place among the team, figure out the best way to use her strengths in conjunction with the strengths of her teammates, and apply exactly what the coach wanted her to do in a way that fit with and contributed to the team as a whole. To do all that successfully, she had to be observant, self-aware, and adjustable—all things that pointed to her adaptability and all things that came in handy for what was required of her next.

The game of soccer has a regular playing time of 90 minutes. Within that hour and a half, there are hundreds of decisions a player needs to make. And fast. It's not a stretch to say that every 10–15 seconds, a soccer player is faced with a choice. Run this way or run that way, cut right or cut left, take a touch with your left foot or right foot, jump into the air to compete for a ball or back off and let her take it. Every decision prompts a chain reaction, resulting in hundreds of new choices. Alex's ability to make split-second decisions and face obstacles in the moment, as they presented themselves, without distraction, had become part of her DNA.

When she was little, she didn't look at the desolate road paved with professional women's soccer hopefuls and feel discouraged. She felt compelled to attempt the improbable.

When she was told she wasn't good enough, she didn't let that determine her worth. She dusted herself off and set out to prove them wrong.

When she went from club team to club team, she didn't let the unknown loom so heavily over her that she felt out of her element or less of a talent than anyone else. She was determined to find where she fit.

When she was faced with decision after decision on the field, she didn't allow apprehension to take over. She felt empowered to make each small decision count.

When Coach Pia Sundhage called her off the bench in the last minutes of the 2011 World Cup qualifying match, she didn't panic or hesitate. She fearlessly, adaptably, and decisively ran onto the field to try to help her team, which as we all know now, she absolutely did.

Alex Morgan is not the only soccer player who's fearless, adaptable, and decisive. In fact, it could be argued that you *must* be those things if you want to succeed in professional soccer. But she is the only player to have her specific history, experiences, obstacles, achievements, opinions, and lessons. And that's where diverse intangibles are formed. Even if people appear to share the same strengths or skills, they're a result of different circumstances. And in the 85th minute of a qualifying match, would you want someone who's fearless because they've repeatedly tried, failed, and kept going or because they're overcompensating for uncertainty? Neither is wrong, but only one would be right for the task at hand.

It's that beautiful and strategic blending of intangibles that Alex has seen repeatedly on the teams for which she's played. Women with their own backgrounds, childhoods, failures, adventures, triumphs, and personalities who came together to offer their uniqueness and create the most effective team they can. And as it turned out, that conglomeration didn't just translate to on-field success but off the field too.

In 2016, Alex and teammates on the USWNT filed a gender-discrimination lawsuit against the US Soccer Federation. Demanding equal pay and gender equality, the female players alleged they were consistently paid less than the players on the men's team and discriminated against because of their gender, despite a strong performance record. What followed were six years of frustrating back-and-forths, full of attorneys, lawmakers, mediations, hearings, media commentary, and additional filings.

While all the female players involved were on the same side and tackling the same issue, they approached it differently. Some were fixers and came at it as a problem to solve. Some were feelers and appealed from a more emotive place. Some were quiet and lent their signatures to the filing but let the others do the talking. Some were outspoken and vocal against the naysayers. Some took it personally, some empathized with the slow wheels of justice, some were fueled by anger. And it took every single type of approach, insight, and behavior for the team to balance each other out and accomplish what they set out to do. In May 2022, Alex and her teammates won a $24 million settlement, guaranteeing equal pay for men and women in friendlies and tournaments, along with a whole host of other measures. It was a historic and transformative win that set up the next generation in ways the current USWNT could have only dreamed of.

For a team to do big things, they can't think small. Yes, intangibles are small, idiosyncratic differences, but they can't be seen in tunnel vision. It requires zooming out to see the big picture, assessing the diverse uniqueness that would positively contribute to the end goal, and finding the right fit among those who present those intangibles. It's a strategic, purpose-driven approach to peak collective performance, which as we now know, has no ceiling.

II

Rethink How You're Going To Do It

3

State of the Union

We're living in a golden age of innovation. Advancements in artificial intelligence, robotics, cloud computing, blockchain, and algorithmic decision making have changed everything from how we interact with each other to how we perform our jobs to how we grow our businesses. In today's economic marketplace, technology is a necessity that's woven into standardized processes across every industry.

But there's a catch.

For all the revolutionary ways technology has impacted the way we work, it's not a one-size-fits-all solution. In the name of business agility, many executives believe technology is yet another must-have tool to acquire, and they're closely watching what the competition is doing to keep up. When it comes to recruitment, however, the idea that implementing technology, adding software, or accessing better data should simply follow a "plug-and-play" approach is overzealous. It's more nuanced than that.

In reality, it's a combination of *both* new technology *and* optimizing people's ability to create value through human touch. It has to be both, and they have to go together. In a world dominated by an either/or mentality, we believe there's a way to strike a balance between adopting innovation, implementing technology, and maintaining a human approach to doing business. Recruitment is all about people.

To think that an advancement in artificial intelligence (AI) or technology will change how we hire in one fell swoop is ambitious at best. And as experts in both, we see that very clearly. AI will transform recruitment, and teams will be able to get far more done than they ever dreamed before. We've seen that firsthand. Technology will make them superhuman at recruitment, able to focus even more on the parts that are distinctly human.

We're not promoting changes to your organizational structure or criticizing your technology management as a whole. We're in the recruitment business, and our insights revolve around optimizing the balance of people, data, and technology to build the right team. It took years of building and scaling an end-to-end recruitment platform for us to hone that balance and see the fundamental value it brings to people on both sides of the process.

But we're getting ahead of ourselves. Before we focus on the right alchemy for recruitment, let's start by looking at the current state of technology and how it's been implemented alongside—or in place of—humans across an array of industries. After all, it's helpful to get a lay of the land before staking a claim.

Best-Laid Plans

In the southern Chinese city of Guangzhou, restaurant chain Heweilai announced an exciting new development: it was going to replace its human staff with robots. Customers would soon deal with artificial intelligence robots programmed to perform all the tasks hosts, waiters, and chefs once did—seat guests, take their orders, prepare and deliver their food, refill drinks, and clear the tables.

With technology and automation progressively affecting jobs, Guangzhou residents weren't surprised as much as they were curious. Patrons flooded the restaurants to see the innovative new gimmick for themselves. They were greeted by a robot that told them a joke as it led them to a table; another robot featured a touchscreen that allowed them to place their orders; yet another robot, programmed to create some 40 dishes, prepared the food; a final robot acted as a bus-boy thanks to its manipulator arm and gesture recognition.

The robotic restaurant was a concept designed to raise efficiency and lower the cost of labor, which averaged close to 10,000 yuan (US $1,465) per month for one worker. What's more, Heweilai would no longer have to think about employees needing vacations or taking sick time. All of this occurred just prior to the Covid-19 pandemic, so combating the extreme labor shortage wasn't a factor—just a prospective problem they'd never have to solve.

Despite initial intrigue from Heweilai's customers, the robots quickly lost their novelty and diners' complaints were wide ranging: special meal requests were lost in translation, drinks and bowls of soup were spilled upon delivery, dishes prepared by the robot chefs were "unpalatable," and the lack of human interaction left guests feeling socially disconnected.

Behind the scenes, Heweilai leadership had their own issues with their new staff. The robots' reliability was low due to technical errors, limited battery life, and restricted programming; the cost per robot, which started at 50,000 yuan, didn't include the high monthly costs of upkeep, repairs, and electricity; and vulnerabilities in the Robot Operating System (ROS) were causing cybersecurity issues and data breaches.

For all the benefits a robotic workforce was supposed to bring to the dining experience, the shortcomings were too glaring. Within a year of Heweilai's announcement, its three "robot restaurants" failed. Two of them closed completely, and one stayed open but re-replaced its staff with humans (though kept one robot to greet customers at the door).

Heweilai wasn't an isolated experiment. Japan's Henn na Hotel, which translates to "Strange Hotel," opened in 2015 with a staff of 250 robots. Recognized by the Guinness Book of World Records as the world's first robot hotel, it featured multilingual robots (one of which was an English-speaking dinosaur robot) at the reception desk that checked guests in. Porter robots sorted and transported luggage

to travelers' rooms. In-room robot assistants helped guests adjust light-
ing, room temperature, and alarm settings. In-room closets doubled as
a laundering service with built-in steamers and hangers that automatically moved around to de-wrinkle clothes and eliminate 99.9%
of germs and bacteria. Separate air-cleaning, window-wiping, and
floor-cleaning robots fulfilled housekeeping duties. Locker room
robots assisted guests hitting the gym. Mobile robots delivered room
service and fresh towels. You get the picture.

But just three years after it opened, the hotel fired half of its robot
"employees" after endless complaints from guests. The robots often
malfunctioned, couldn't answer basic questions, and could only travel
on flat surfaces, severely limiting their ability to access all 100 rooms.
Guests reported their robot room assistants thought snoring sounds
were commands and would wake them up repeatedly during the
night to ask, "Sorry, I couldn't catch that. Could you repeat your
request?" Others complained that the robots were unable to perform
simple tasks that a smartphone could handle, like when the robot
concierge wasn't able to provide guests with information around
flight schedules or tourist attractions that Siri took only seconds to
produce. And the droids at reception couldn't understand guests'
names or make copies of their passports without human help.

It turned out robots weren't the best at hospitality.

What many companies miss is that becoming forward-thinking
often requires us to become more human, not less. Robot restaurants
and hotels are innovative and exciting concepts, but putting everything in the hands of AI caused product quality and customer satisfaction to suffer. Technology can make things more efficient, but that
doesn't necessarily mean more effective. In other words, just because
you can doesn't mean you should.

The Beginning of the End

Efficiency and productivity are crucial to business growth; the amount
of time and effort it takes to carry out a host of responsibilities can be

the determining factor between forward progress and stagnation. Consequently, much emphasis has been put on increasing the quality and quantity of outputs without increasing costs. This dilemma has been around as long as work itself and, throughout history, important innovations have attempted to solve it.

Two hundred years ago, our country's economy revolved around agriculture. What we needed most was to continue producing successful farmers in order to grow, feed, and sustain a new nation, and because farming wasn't the technologically efficient machine it is today, doing so required a lot of people. Basically everyone. This meant large families were the order of the day, and from the time a kid could carry a bucket, they were apprenticed in the how-tos of operating a farm or supporting farmers. Even those who didn't rely on the farm into their adulthood were usually trained to carry out another vocation indirectly supporting the tools, products, and industry of farming.

Agricultural employment remained prominent in the United States through the 1800s and into the turn of the century, but an underlying swell was rising: mechanization.

John Froelich built the first lightweight, gas-driven tractor in America in 1892. By 1901, Dan Albone had constructed a lightweight general purpose tractor on the foundation of an internal combustion engine. Fifty years before that, in the 1840s, English agricultural entrepreneur John Bennet Lawes began investing resources in the possibilities of organic and artificial fertilizer to increase crop yields. By 1910, the work of chemists Carl Bosh and Fritz Huber had commercialized the process of synthesizing ammonium nitrate to create synthetic fertilizer that was far more effective than previous fertilizers.[1]

These innovations increased agricultural productivity while decreasing the workforce required to get the work done. Hands-on farming became less and less necessary, and by 1911, many farmworkers had become factory workers, standing in assembly lines and repeating the same tasks over and over in order to eventually produce what we needed to thrive: machinery, engines, planes, trains, and automobiles. With this increased conformity, production and output soared. (For perspective, when Henry Ford first conceived the Model T, it took 13 hours to assemble. Within five years, he was turning out a vehicle every 93 minutes.)[2]

The assembly line did away with the craftsman-like approach where one highly skilled person or a small group of highly skilled people would perform all necessary tasks for production. Instead, each person could now perform a relatively simple task in just about every large-scale operation. And through that subdivision, it became possible to reduce the complexity of each task to the point where some tasks could be automated. Enter robotics.

First commercially used on assembly lines in the early 1960s, most robots featured hydraulic or pneumatic arms, were powered by a single electric motor, and were primarily used for heavy lifting. Soon, they were welding, painting, gluing, assembling, tending to the machines, and transporting material, thanks to a fully electrically driven and microprocessor-controlled robot that debuted in 1973. These types of advances in technology, including the emergence of commercial computers, marked the transition from the industrial to the information age.

Computers had actually been around for decades. From as far back as the 1930s, mainframe computers were used by entities like the US government to conduct census counts and create strategies for defense systems. The computers weighed five tons, filled an entire room, and cost about $200,000 to build.[3] With the progression of hardware—vacuum tubes to transistors, integrated circuits to silicon computer chips—a veritable explosion of personal computers occurred in the mid-1970s and steadily became a staple of work-places everywhere.

You would be hard-pressed to find someone who doesn't think the advent of computers made their work life easier. Routine tasks, from dictation to typing, were suddenly streamlined; computerized telephone systems meant that operators or attendants didn't have to rely on switchboards to establish connections; paper ledgers, and the recurrent inaccuracies that went along with them, were replaced by accounting software. Technical capabilities grew in conjunction with improved data storage, memory, and speed, and by the 1980s (and certainly the 1990s), end-to-end digitization of work was the new normal.

While technology and automation aren't mutually exclusive, the prevalence of technology in the workplace resulted in many automated processes. Theoretically, automation substituted human labor when a worker's tasks were routine and codifiable, and complemented labor by allowing workers to be more productive in the areas humans could excel in, from idea generation to problem solving to pattern recognition—all of which constituted computers' weaknesses.

In recent decades, technology has closed the gap even more. Statistical machine learning methods learn patterns from data. They are rooted in statistics, which is all about modeling uncertainty with mathematics. Computers can consume more data than humans, and statistical processes we can model can be executed on computers. In the past 30 years, machine learning and modern AI methods have taken these ideas to an extreme. Powerful theories from statistics and computer science have given way to an explosion of practical methods for reasoning about uncertainty, in a way that can be executed on a staggering number of problems, by computers. The vast amount and speed of computation, storage, and connectivity at our fingertips today has opened up new possibilities. Machine learning models with billions of parameters are common now; they were barely conceivable, except at the biggest companies, 10 years ago. There is still a long way to go toward making these systems interpretable, safe, and even understandable. And that's a place where we still need human judgment, and to improve the technology. Large communities are working hard at it. But there is no doubt that the progress is very real, and for knowledge workers, it will continue to touch our lives in nearly every way.

Projections of historical trends, like that of Moore's Law, which observes that the number of transistors in a dense integrated circuit doubles about every two years, have long forecasted the rapid change in information processing technologies. And newer philosophies, like the Law of Accelerating Returns, which points to the positive feed-back loop of evolution and improvement of processes over time, describe the exponential growth trajectory of technology. There is also the belief that whenever a technology approaches some kind of barrier, a new technology will be invented to allow us to cross that barrier. Does that mean computers' weaknesses could ultimately become strengths?

Man Versus Machine

Let's talk about games for a moment. Games are fixed worlds with a relatively small set of rules. They are a bounded domain where people can play, within the rules, toward a goal. And of course, computers can play games too. So, a common way to measure productivity of computers toward becoming human-like in their ability to reason, is to teach it games, and go heads up against the best humans. Computers are now superior to humans on several games, most famously (and in increasing order of difficulty) backgammon, chess, and Go. It is the story of humans, computers, and chess that we want to focus on.

Chess is a game of strategy. Two players, one board, sixteen chess pieces each, and in order to win, you must have a better plan of action than your opponent. There are so many possible ways any one game can go—more than nine million after the first three moves—which enthralls the estimated 800 million people who play chess world-wide.[4] But despite the seemingly endless ways to approach the game and the number of active players, playing chess and mastering chess are two different things.

The grandmaster title is the highest title awarded in chess, and as of 2020, there were only 1,721 of them in the world. A recent analysis estimated how many hours of play it takes to reach the coveted des-ignation: 12,480. Further data broke it down into how many specific games one needs to play to become a grandmaster, which ranged from 2,831 to 18,106 games. Suffice it to say, mastering chess is a huge time commitment, though not everyone who puts in the time is assured a title. That's because in addition to devoting their time, elite chess players have distinct skills that prove crucial to mastery.[5]

Winning the invisible psychological battle with the person sitting across the chessboard requires uncanny amounts of focus, memory, studiousness, self-analysis, pattern recognition, and neural efficiency. That last one was the subject of a study that compared the brains of grandmasters and amateurs. Researchers found that chess experts had reduced gray matter volume in the subcortical brain structures in charge of memory and reinforcement learning. These concepts exist both in neuroscience but also AI, and make their way into AI methods through computational approaches that call out to our primitive understanding of how the brain works. The authors associated this reduction or "neuronal pruning" with the elimination of redundant or unused synapses, otherwise known as neural efficiency.[6] Layman's terms: through long-term intensive chess training, the brain underwent structural and functional changes that allowed it to function in a more concentrated and focused way. Humans are amazing!

Not part of the study, though certainly could have been, is Garry Kasparov. A Russian chess grandmaster and former World Chess Champion, he's considered one of the greatest positional geniuses in chess history. He became the youngest ever undisputed champion in 1985 at 22 years old and continued his reign as the number one player in the world for the next 15 years. Well, except for a few days in 1997 when his remarkable human abilities were put to the test against a computer.

Deep Blue was a chess-playing expert system run on a unique purpose-built IBM supercomputer. It had two customized VLSI-technology move generator chips and was capable of searching up to 200 million moves per second. But even with the most sophisticated programming available at the time, critics figured there was no way it could solve the complex, strategic, and intuitive game of chess; over the years, many computers had taken on chess masters, and the computers always lost.

Before 1949, computers could execute commands, but they couldn't remember what they did as they weren't able to store the commands. That all changed in 1950 when mathematician Alan Turing, who was working on software for one of the earliest stored-program computers, wrote an amazing paper called "Computing Machinery and Intelligence" which introduced the concept of artificial intelligence—as in, can we program machines to think like a human? Five years later, the first AI program was presented at Dartmouth Summer Research Project on Artificial Intelligence (DSPRAI), an event that catalyzed AI research for the next few decades.

By the time Kasparov and Deep Blue sat at a chessboard with cameras rolling and millions watching, IBMers knew the odds of Deep Blue winning weren't certain. But after almost 50 years of developing adequate computing technology and formulating sufficient chess-playing strategies, they felt the science was solid. And as it turned out, it was. After Kasparov won the first game and lost the second, the following three were draws. But then, Deep Blue won the final game, taking the match and making history as the first computer to beat a world champion in a six-game match under regular time controls.

Deep Blue's win was seen as symbolically significant, a sign that artificial intelligence was catching up to human intelligence. And the advancements in computing that followed soon thereafter did nothing to quash the assumption. Dragon Systems' speech recognition software was implemented in Windows. Apple's Siri understood and responded to spoken requests and became standard on iPhones. Google's search algorithms were able to make accessible to everyone on Earth, in any language, a vast, ever-changing quantity of data on the public internet; it could translate most language pairs into one another with remarkable accuracy. IBM's Watson combined technologies for natural language processing, hypothesis generation, and evidence-based learning and won *Jeopardy!* against two of its greatest human contestants. OpenAI's GPT generator models would complete strings of text in ways we couldn't have imagined just several years ago. Computers would learn to write descriptions of images, based on the image alone, and generate images based on text descriptions of them. It seemed there wasn't a problem machines couldn't handle or a level of proficiency they couldn't achieve.

All of these problems have a common thread: They require a huge amount of data, a clear way to write the prediction problem the computer is solving that is also expressed in the data, and a succinct algorithm for training the computer to model parameters against that same data set. It is a statistical process. Computers learn by tuning parameters to fit the data, with enough expressive power to make good predictions when new data comes in.

Just as factory jobs were eliminated in the twentieth century by new assembly-line robots, rapid advancements in artificial intelligence and machine learning seem to be contending with human-centric abilities and vying for jobs. While most technological shifts are assumed to disrupt low-skilled labor markets, the proliferation of AI technology progressively seems to be disrupting skilled knowledge workers whose jobs involve data-driven decision-making. Is it only a matter of time before humans are phased out of the workforce altogether? It's a hot topic for debate, but these debates tend to stray from the practical realities. We don't sense impending doom. The amount we understand about these technologies is still so primitive. There's a lot to learn. We sense opportunity.

Creative Destruction

When Henry Ford's assembly line revolutionized the automobile manufacturing industry, it displaced older markets and forced many laborers out of work. That observation prompted Austrian economist Joseph Schumpeter to coin the term "creative destruction" to describe the disruptive process of transformation that accompanies innovation. This evolutionary process—that is, a new invention destroying what came before it—is a necessary component of doing business. Not the deliberate replacement of human jobs, but the embracing of competition and innovation as essential for economic growth.

Companies that once revolutionized and dominated new industries—for example, Xerox in copiers or Polaroid in instant photography—have seen their profits fall and their dominance vanish as rivals launched improved designs or cut manufacturing costs. In technology, the cassette tape replaced the 8-track, only to be replaced by the compact disc, which was undercut by downloads to MP3 players, which is now being superseded by web-based streaming services.

The information age has seen a transformation of where data lives. Thousands of years ago, knowledge lived in people's brains and was shared through story, relayed live. Writing shifted time and space for stories, as they could be recorded on paper, and then read anytime. The printing press made the process of writing faster and transferable. Tapes and movie reels shifted information further toward electronics, through magnetic bits, and could communicate rich audio and video anytime, anywhere, with the right player. And of course, internet connectivity and purely electronic encoding of information has gotten us to where we are today.

Without the old, there would be no new. We can mourn what was, or we can appreciate how it laid the groundwork for what is and still could be. That is the essence of creative destruction: phasing out the old technologies and inviting in the new to develop better products or services. Subsequently, it hurts those who remain stagnant and rewards those who are able to adapt around transformations.

In business we talk about pivots a lot. These are really like evolutionary steps. Businesses are just solutions to problems people have, built by other people, over time. So, it stands to reason that when the world changes, so do businesses. Shifting to a new strategy, product, or market to accommodate changing circumstances, which can range from customer preferences to market demand to technological advances, is natural. We've all heard the famous accounts of companies that refused to adapt or were too late to do so: Blockbuster,

Toys "R" Us, Pan Am, Borders Books, General Motors, and Kodak, to name a few. Then there are the success stories, the companies that pivoted their focus and became industry giants.

Starbucks started out selling espresso machines. Twitter was a platform for finding podcasts. Nintendo produced vacuum cleaners. YouTube was a video dating site (unofficial first slogan: "Tune in, hook up"). Nokia began as a single-factory wood pulp mill, then manufactured rubber boots. Samsung was a company that exported dried fish and flour from Korea to China. Groupon was a social good fundraising site that ran on a "tipping point" system, where a cause would only receive funding once the pledged donations reached a certain number.[7]

Pivoting can safeguard or revitalize an organization, and nothing revealed the essential value of the pivot more than the pandemic. The crisis forced companies into massive experiments in how to be more nimble, flexible, and fast. And to do so successfully, it requires a team that works the same way.

Health care startup Curative launched in January 2020 with the goal of improving the health outcomes of patients with sepsis, the body's extreme response to infection. But within weeks, there seemed to be a more urgent medical challenge: providing Covid-19 testing. We helped the company, a client of ours, jump from seven employees to 7,000 workers to adjust to their new direction, which was just the beginning of their impressive adaptation. To accommodate the influx of staff, Curative built whole mock-lab setups where they could train up to 50 cohorts at a time; when the lab software system they purchased from an outside vendor couldn't keep up with the amount of tests, they built their own software; when swab supplies were tight, they repurposed swabs meant for electronics manufacturing (they were just as sterile!); during a statewide deployment of one million test kits in nursing and group homes in Florida, Curative ran out of barcode scanners, and when the United Parcel Service, which was distributing its test kits, told the company it had run out of vans, Curative hired private couriers.[8]

Another successful pivoter was longtime toy manufacturer Mattel. Along with most other toymakers, it knew that many families needed new ways to keep kids busy while school closed its doors, but Mattel surpassed competition by creating a brand-new product that no one else had: key worker–themed action figures. The "#ThankYouHeroes" collection included nurses, doctors, grocery store workers, delivery drivers, and EMTs, and all net proceeds went to #FirstRespondersFirst, an initiative created to support health care workers serving on the frontlines. Mattel saw its sales soar 47% in Q1 2021, exceeding all expectations from Wall Street.[9]

The travel industry undoubtedly took a hit during the pandemic. Vacation plans were paused, work conferences canceled, business travel restricted. Many hotels across the country either shut down entirely or had extremely low occupancy, mainly providing rooms for stranded tourists, journalists, hospital workers, or pilots. But one hotel chain, Red Roof, switched up its business model and offered day rates for remote workers to use rooms as makeshift workspaces. They implemented a "Work Under Our Roof" program where workers who didn't have at-home offices or spaces conducive to working from home could pay low rates for a quiet room, and "coworkers" (one well-behaved domestic cat or dog) were welcome to come free of charge.[10]

When times change, and they always do, the teams that are willing to course-correct are often the ones that survive. The individuals who get creative and move quickly figure out the best course of action. They evolve together as a functioning unit to match what the world needs. The *who* figures out the *how*. Whether we're talking about global pandemics, recessions, market saturation, or ever-evolving technology, adaptability can mean stability.

Augmented Intelligence: The Other AI

There's an African American folk hero named John Henry who worked as a "steel-driving man"—a man tasked with hammering a steel drill into rock to make holes for explosives during the construction of railroad tunnels. According to legend, Henry was the strongest, fastest, and most powerful man working on the Big Bend Tunnel in West Virginia in the 1880s. In what would become one of the earliest narratives of pitting humanity against technology, his prowess as a steel driver was measured in a race against a steam-powered rock drilling machine.

As the story goes, Henry used two 10-pound hammers, one in each hand, and pounded the drill so fast and so hard that he drilled a 14-foot hole into the rock. The machine was only able to drill nine feet. Henry beat the steam drill but died of exhaustion immediately afterwards, hammer in hand.

Symbolic in many cultural movements, including labor movements and the Civil Rights Movement, John Henry most notably represents "the dignity of a human being against the degradations of the machine age."[11] This competitive rhetoric seems standard now, and reiterates the longtime dramatic rivalry between man and technology. But why does it have to be so divisive?

We're not discounting the adverse impact that tech—specifically automation—can have on human jobs; there's no denying that some roles will no longer require humans in the future. The World Economic Forum predicted in 2020 that workplace automation would disrupt 85 million jobs globally by 2025, a faster-than-expected increase due to Covid-19. But it also predicted that in the same time span, the robot revolution would create 97 million new jobs that are more adapted to the division of labor between humans, machines, and algorithms.[12] Perfect segue.

A century after John Henry's poetic justice, grandmaster Garry Kasparov found himself the modern-day symbol after losing the chess match to Deep Blue. As the self-professed "first knowledge worker whose job was threatened by a machine,"[13] he surprised people with his attitude post-loss: if you can't beat 'em, join 'em.

Kasparov ultimately saw artificial intelligence as an opportunity for collaboration, not a future overlord or oppressor. He wondered if he could play *with* a computer to combine their strengths—human intuition plus machine's calculations, human strategy plus machine's tactics, human experience plus machine's memory. Could it be the most perfect game ever played?

One year later, Kasparov partnered with a PC running chess software in a match against Veselin Topalov, a Bulgarian whom he had beaten 4–0 just a month earlier. This time, with both players supported by computers, the match ended in a 3–3 draw. It appeared the use of a PC nullified the calculative and strategic advantages Kasparov usually displayed over his opponents.

The match provided an important illustration of how humans might work with AI. After the match, Kasparov felt that the use of a PC allowed him to focus more on strategic planning while the machine took care of calculations. But he stressed that simply putting together the best human player and best PC did not ensure perfect games. And importantly, it made Topalov competitive with Kasparov, when that was not the case previously. Like with human teams, the power of working with an AI comes from how the person and computer complement each other; the best players and most powerful AIs partnering up wouldn't necessarily produce the best results.

In 2005, an online chess-playing site hosted what it called a "freestyle" chess tournament in which anyone could compete in teams with other players or computers. What made this competition interesting was that several groups of grandmasters working with computers also participated. Predictably, most people expected that one of the grandmasters in combination with a supercomputer would dominate the tournament—but that's not what happened. The tournament was won by a pair of amateur American chess players operating three ordinary PCs at the same time. Their skill of coaching their machines effectively counteracted the superior chess knowledge of their grandmaster opponents and much greater computational power.

The surprising result highlights an important lesson: the process of how players and computers interact determines how efficient the partnership will be.

That's exactly how we feel about the interaction of humans and machines in the workforce. There are circumstances where machines can augment human labor (and vice versa), leading to complementary and mutually empowering relationships that are efficient and effective. While artificial intelligence is usually seen as an autonomous system, the reality will not be so binary. Machines and humans will work together to enhance, rather than replace, humans for particular tasks. Think about the experience of Googling something. You try a search, learn, and then improve your search. You work with Google—it learns how to get better from you, and you learn how to use it, in the ways it is most effective. The idea of methodical interplay between technology and people to influence processes is, in our opinion, just as powerful as artificial intelligence.

The Ultimate Merger

Some of the most innovative and resourceful marriages between tech and humans have happened organically.

When Hurricane Katrina struck New Orleans, low-lying places were under so much water that people had to scramble to attics and rooftops for safety. Despondent residents, who needed evacuation and called 911, were patched through to Coast Guard radio dispatchers. The callers were asked to identify their exact locations and they responded with their addresses. But this presented a problem for the Coast Guard navigation systems, because they were almost universally deployed somewhere off the coast to help capsized boats, cargo ships, and offshore oil rigs. In other words, locations that used latitude and longitude coordinates instead of street addresses.

That's when helicopter dispatchers downloaded Google Earth, a technology that had been released only two months earlier. Suddenly, they could enter a street address, and by simply rolling over the house with the mouse, they could get the exact coordinates and elevation of the rooftop and then radio the information to the nearest helicopter for rescue. And thanks to the up-to-date imagery, the dispatcher was even able to tell the pilot additional situational information, such as fallen trees and downed power lines. The detailed, elevated views were generated from the newest technology. The key physiographic observations were assessed and communicated by human dispatchers. Together, they helped the Coast Guard save more than 400 lives.[14]

Other effective partnerships between tech and humans are more deliberate, often featuring the more traditional robot-human relationship (we acknowledge the irony since there's really nothing traditional about it). For example, a German factory that produces Adidas running shoes uses robotic technology to make the shoe while humans oversee the assembly process and testing during pilot phases. This may seem like a standard partnership seen in plenty of manufacturing processes, but the coolest thing about this endeavor is how intertwined the collaboration is from beginning to end.

Traditional fabric manufacturing usually only allows for threads to be placed horizontally or vertically. But Adidas' computer and sports scientists spent four years creating a technology that sees a robot quickly place more than a thousand individual threads at different angles across the material part of the shoe. Different yarns used in different sections fulfill different purposes: the stiffest thread is used in the heel region, while fewer, breathable threads are used in the middle of the foot toward the toes.

The company built custom robotics and software to create the stringy canvas by conducting high-resolution scans of how runners' feet move as they travel. The design combines behavioral data, such as how fast people are running and the conditions they're running in, and dimensional analysis, including how the foot's movement helps position where each of the threads go. A team of humans tweak and add extra expertise to the process, with modifications based on how comfortable the shoes are. They then go into the software and "manipulate" individual threads or grouping of threads.

During the earliest prototypes, Adidas staffers spent entire days hand-placing threads to see if their idea could work. That, obviously, wasn't scalable. By using robots, 10 different spools of thread go through a central threading system to automatically create the upper part of the shoe from the digital designs in a matter of minutes. This makes it easier to test new designs with different thread positioning and also has the benefit of being able to produce shoes at scale. It's a prime example of how to attain efficiency and productivity by using a methodical combination of tech and humans.

But let's go one step further. Instead of the familiar scenario of robots and humans working on separate tasks with little to no direct interaction, there's an augmented option: cobots, or collaborative robots, which operate in conjunction with, and in close proximity to, humans. Instead of replacing humans with autonomous counterparts, cobots augment and enhance human capabilities.

Invented in the mid-1990s by professors at Northwestern University, cobots took off in the last decade and are different from traditional industrial robots in a number of ways. For one, they're safer. They don't need isolated areas to function; they can share the same physical space with human employees without any danger thanks to external sensors that allow them to slow down or stop when a person approaches. Plus, cobots' joints are force limited, meaning each joint is equipped with a force sensor which adds a quick reaction in case of collision, making the cobot stop. Two, they're smaller and lighter and often have two arms which aid in performing delicate tasks like assembling small parts, tightening screws, or bin picking. And three, they're more intelligent than their programmable counterparts. Cobots are built on behaviors; they're goal-directed computational entities that are focused on an outcome so they think at a more abstract level as opposed to just moving from one coordinate to the next.

Cobots are mainly used in the industries you'd expect— manufacturing, food processing, construction, health care—and work side-by-side with personnel. At a Ford factory in Germany, for example, cobots work on Fiesta models to fit shock absorbers. Since working with heavy, air-powered tools attached overhead is a hard task that necessitates exceptional strength, precision, and stamina, cobots are

installed on a mount and take care of the heavy lifting part of the duty
while the humans perform the others. Similarly, at a BMW factory in
the UK, cobots are used in the riveting process. Whereas the task used
to be performed entirely by workers—they would first load the rivets
and then do the actual riveting—the human employee now loads one
side of the jig while the cobot begins work on the other. In the med-
tech industry, a Minnesota-based medical manufacturer employs
cobots to pick-and-place intricate injection moldings from the mold-
ing site to the trimming area to the human operator for the
next phase.[15]

These machines are ideal for merging the work of humans and
technology. They focus on collaboration and teamwork, allowing the
human coworker to focus on tasks that require greater dexterity and
cognitive abilities than the cobot possesses, which focuses on repetitive tasks.

Cobots perfectly encapsulate our process: a precise ratio of humans
and technology that allows us to hand off the tedious to allow time
for the meaningful. And they are really just more illustrative examples
of work that is already happening. The computers that make good
chess players compete with grandmasters are cobots. Google is an
incredible resource that makes expertise on almost any subject accessible to anyone on Earth, at any time. It will happen all over our lives
in the years to come. As machines are capable of doing more and
more, we can argue that it's decreasing human jobs, or we can appreciate that it's allowing humans to focus on more meaningful work.
Instead of dehumanizing us, using tech in a smart way can actually
help rehumanize work.

Consider the example of Clara, a virtual teammate that helps
schedule meetings and manage calendars. It blends machine intelligence with human support to automate repetitive tasks; a conversational intelligence trained on high-quality data, labeled by the
distributed efforts of an expert team 24 hours a day. Clara adapts to
users' workflows, syncs with calendars for scheduling and follow-ups,
and interacts with everyone in natural language via email. The human
in the loop ensures speed, accuracy, and data refinement. The product

itself is a perfect blend of tech and people, but its benefits are entirely focused on the user, saving people countless hours of minutiae and massive amounts of brainpower. In this way, Clara doesn't subtract from the human experience but rather adds to it.

Tech that's utilized in an astute way makes decisions *instead of* and *for* people. While some may argue that workers' best interests are at odds with tech—that humans and machines are in direct competition—we believe that's a false dichotomy that's uninformed and outdated. Smart tech and humans are not competing with one another; they are complementary, but only when the tech is used well.

We'll show you exactly what we mean.

4

On the Shoulders of Giants

There was a great first-mover movement in the early 2000s. The idea was that the initial ("first-moving") significant occupant in a given market gained an advantageous and perhaps insurmountable market position just by being first. The theory has legs. Sony was the first mover in personal stereos, Coca-Cola in soft drinks, Hoover in vacuum cleaners, Amazon in online books sales. These well-known examples have enjoyed considerable success, but it didn't work that way for a lot of other ventures.

Dumont led the way in selling TV sets when they were new devices, but the company lost out to latecomers like RCA and Motorola. Ampex had a commanding position in video recorders for two decades until Sony took over. Sidecar was the pioneer of ride-sharing yet Uber was the one to dominate the market. Netscape was the first to market an internet browser until their stock price plummeted following the rise of Microsoft's Explorer.

If being "the first" doesn't give you the upper hand, what does? If the preceding examples are any indication, innovation isn't enough. Nor is displacing incumbents, creating new markets, or pushing an entire industry forward. No, companies who find long-lasting success do so through identifying gaps and ramping up execution in those areas, finding opportunities that are disguised as voids and then throwing ingenuity and resources into solving those problems.

That's what Google did.

In 1998, there were numerous search engines: Excite, WebCrawler, AltaVista, Lycos, America Online, Yahoo!, HotBot, MSN, and Ask Jeeves, just to name a few. Though, as you may or may not remember, none of them had very good search capabilities; they weren't that thorough or user-friendly and they had a lot going on. They were littered with ads. They suffered from spam and relevancy issues. Some wanted you to edit results. Others wanted you to narrow down your results through the use of keywords. But then Google came along and eclipsed every last one of them.

There were multiple reasons why Google was such a superior option. For one, Google ranked search results using a trademarked algorithm called PageRank, which assigned each web page a relevancy score, so the odds of them pulling up what you were looking for far exceeded their competitors. Two, it used query expansion techniques to decipher what users were *really* searching for, as opposed to just relying on what they entered into the search bar. Three, it featured a search bar and little else, making it simple to use and abundantly clear to the user that searching was the primary function of the site. And four, it understood better than any other company that a search engine's sole purpose was to get rid of users as quickly as possible.

Search engines aren't made to be destinations; they're specifically designed to act as a middleman between your question and the site that has the answer. Whichever site will get you to your destination quickest, no matter the complexity of your query, is the one you'd find most useful, right? No other search engine has been able to master that concept like Google. From the get-go, they rebelled against the orthodox view that "stickiness" was crucial to a website's success.

In the 1990s, most internet executives believed that for a web service to be profitable, it had to be, in essence, like a TV show—meaning that it had to hold its users' attention long enough to deliver advertising. This ability to hold attention was known as "stickiness" and was the most desired web metric at the time. Just as TV viewers would endure commercials in order to watch great programming, so the execs reasoned, they'd endure advertisements in order to get their queries answered for free. And the longer users stayed on the page, the more advertising a search engine could sell.

Google refused to play that game, and in their early years, it was often to their detriment. When they tried to sell their technology to Excite, the deal was a nonstarter. Excite's CEO felt that if they were to host a search engine that instantly gave people the information they sought, the users would leave the site immediately afterwards. Since ad revenue at Excite came from people staying on the site, using Google's technology would be counterproductive. When explaining his refusal to make a deal, the CEO told Google execs that he wanted Excite's search engine to only be 80% as good as the other search engines. He was more concerned about generating revenue than search efficiency.[1]

It's no wonder Google has proven to be the one with staying power. Its fresh and independent thinking has translated to an ever-increasing dominance of the search engine market; as of 2022, Google had acquired 92.5% of it.[2] Further, it proves the power of prioritizing customer value above all else—and at all costs, much to the chagrin of advertisers. It also proves that by disrupting the status quo, you can solve big problems and accommodate even bigger needs.

Google found a distinct edge and used it to produce something that would be uniquely valuable for consumers. Excessive ads, biased or irrelevant website results, and chaotic designs were the norm for search engines, and we were just the fools who didn't know there was a better way. When Google launched and provided us with a tasteful, fast platform and quality search capabilities, it shifted our expectations. It showed us what was possible.

What's particularly notable is that Google didn't conceptually change the search engine, it simply molded established technology

into a more user-friendly and useful form. It didn't completely eliminate the use of ads, but it enabled a new means of connecting users
and advertisers by prioritizing only relevant ads. It didn't just rely on
keywords and Boolean logic, it methodically predicted what users
actually meant. It saw where other search engines fell short, reverse-
engineered a better product, and respected its users enough to make
the whole thing about their experience.

And Google didn't stop there.

Circa 1997, MSN, AOL, and Yahoo! became more than search
engines when they added an email service. The experience was the
same for all users. Inboxes were overtaken by spam. There was no easy
way to search your inbox or file messages away. You had to constantly
delete emails to stay under the storage limit.

In 2004, Google launched Gmail, changing everything we
thought we knew about the email experience. It blocked spam before
it ever reached your inbox. It had the power of Google Search built
right in and grouped messages into conversation threads, making it
easier to find and reply to them. It stored 1GB of data for free, nearly
100 times what other providers supplied. In the years to come, it
released more never-before-seen email features like autocomplete,
to-do lists, themes, and the tabbed inbox. It also rolled out products
like Google Calendar, Travel, Maps, Translate, Chrome, G Suite (now
Workspace), and Photos, connecting all facets of our lives into one
seamless user experience.

Google tied things together and solved problems we didn't even
know we had. We had no idea how valuable it would be to book a
flight and have the details automatically appear in our calendar. Or go
into Google Photos, search "dog," and find every picture of Rover
we've ever taken. Or drop a pin and give someone our exact GPS
coordinates. We didn't know what we were missing until it arrived,
and there was no going back.

Google saw the forest for the trees. By looking at the landscape as
a whole, it was able to identify the gaps. By thinking like a user, it
determined which features and products would actually help in

people's everyday lives. By thinking like a tech company, it strategized relevant and reliable solutions. By prioritizing best-in-class technology and customer value, it became one of the most trusted companies in the world.

The Office

We think of old recruiting methods in the same way we think of old search engines: not efficient, not user-friendly, and not good at understanding what you're *really* looking for. We don't fault old recruiting methods though. They're . . . old. They go all the way back to 1650.

The first officially documented recruitment agency was started by Henry Robinson. He was a noted religious dissenter, philosopher, merchant, writer, and sometimes government official when he opened the brand new and unusual business on Threadneedle Street in London: the Office of Addresses and Encounters. At the Office, for a modest fee of sixpence, individuals could record their addresses and what services they could offer, and businesses could list what needs they might have. (For the same fee, the Office also provided answers to other types of queries: lodgers could find accommodations, hard-to-find merchandise was matched with buyers, and the lovelorn could find companionship. So in addition to recruitment, Robinson basically invented Airbnb, eBay, and Match.com.)

Two hundred years later, specialized and privately owned agencies began to pop up. In 1883, John Gabbitas recruited schoolmasters for public schools in England. In 1890, the Mrs. A. E. Johnson Employment Agency hired lady's maids, parlor maids, and footmen for the upper class in the United States (including Roosevelt, Carnegie, and Rockefeller). In 1893, Fred Winslow started an engineering agency. In 1906, Katherine Felton opened an agency after the San Francisco earthquake and fire, which killed more than 3,000 people and destroyed over 80% of the city.[3]

But what most would consider modern-day recruitment started during World War II when agencies were set up to fill gaps left in the workplace after men were called to join the war efforts. With so many vacancies to fill, staffing agencies and professional job recruiters mined a gap, helping to match individuals to suitable positions. After the war, returning soldiers needed to find employment and large corporations were growing steadily with the return of the American consumer. The result was a hiring frenzy that led to even more agencies.

To find or publicize a job, newspaper advertisements or physical job boards were standard. Agencies would scour these resources on behalf of job seekers, and also cold-call companies to see about their hiring needs. Candidates were encouraged to write résumés, which needed to include specifics like age, weight, height, marital status, race, religion, and health conditions. While résumés used to just be formalities written on scrap pieces of paper, by 1960 they were expected and people agonized over everything from whether they should lie about their singledom to how to get enough copies if they didn't have access to a photocopier.

Fun fact: Leonardo da Vinci is widely credited with drafting the first "résumé" in 1482 in the form of a letter written to the Duke of Milan to gain his patronage. Proving he was as skillful in his job search prowess as his artistic talents, da Vinci made sure the letter focused on the strengths he had that were most clearly aligned with the Duke's needs. Among them, the ability to make covered chariots safe and unattackable and construct an endless variety of bridges.[4]

The 1970s and 1980s saw the number of recruitment agencies climb, some of which are still around today. Companies like Randstad, Adecco, and Robert Half wrote the proverbial book on process and approach: binders full of job listings, filing cabinets full of résumés, and persistent cold calling. Applying and hiring was done in person, with typewritten résumés in hand, and recruiters had to keep track of a slew of predigital paperwork.

That all changed, at least for the most part, with the emergence of computers. Typewriters were swapped for word processors, résumés could now be faxed, line printers and dot matrix printers could connect to computers via parallel ports, and sending electronic mail was possible if the sender and recipient were on the same network. When it came to recruitment, the initial stages of high-touch versus high-tech had officially begun.

The Boom

The 1990s were a busy time: the internet and World Wide Web went public, pop culture took flight, we vowed our loyalty to either *Seinfeld* or *Friends*, fast food was supersized, and online job searching became a thing.

Monster and HotJobs were the first major players in the online recruitment space, basically digital versions of the classified section. They aggregated job postings in one place—aptly called job boards—and allowed candidates to upload their résumés and apply for infinite jobs in one click. And thanks to their commercials during Super Bowl XXXIII in 1999, lightbulbs went off for job seekers everywhere and searching for jobs on the internet became a phenomenon.

Monster spent $4 million for three 30-second TV ads, which was 15% of its annual marketing budget. HotJobs spent 64% of its $2.5 million revenue on its one ad spot. Risky moves considering Super Bowl commercials traditionally featured beer, car, and credit card companies, and had only ever featured one website-specific ad before (for Autobytel, a car buying site). But it paid off. Monster went from doing 600 job searches per minute to almost 2,900 per minute while HotJobs reported a fivefold increase in traffic after the game.[5]

With growing popularity, more job search sites followed, many with their own niche. Indeed was equivalent to a talent version of Google, a metasearch engine for job boards. CareerPath.com aggregated the classified sections from six major newspapers, including the *Los Angeles Times*, *Chicago Tribune*, and the *Washington Post*. Dice.com focused on jobs in the technology field. CareerBuilder sold software to companies for listing job openings on their websites. Headhunter.net provided recruiting services to employers and recruitment advertising agencies. TheLadders.com focused exclusively on

$100k+ salaried positions. LinkedIn was the Facebook for work, using social media for professional networking.

This eruption of websites exposed job seekers to more opportunities than they would encounter offline; it allowed them to become passive seekers who could post a résumé and let employers find them, or browse and apply to a bunch of jobs all at one time. Employers thought they were in an equally advantageous position with their influx of candidates and the ability to pick the best in class. But it wasn't quite the matchmaking solution everyone hoped.

With access to a myriad of centralized job postings, many passive candidates applied to jobs for which they were unqualified. There seemed to be a consensus among them that the most qualified candidates were already killing it at the job they were in, giving the passive candidate the confidence to aspirationally apply for roles despite being ill-matched.

On the other side of the equation, hiring managers were sorting through thousands of unsuitable candidates, leading many to wonder if having a job board full of people who other companies hadn't already snatched up meant they were picking from a weaker pool. Their frustration over not finding enough qualified talent was second only to their feelings of being overwhelmed while trying to manage the amount of incoming applications.

That torrent of applicants popularized Applicant Tracking Systems (ATS), databases that could process, save, and run basic screening on incoming résumés. They provided organization, and many of the systems allowed for more efficient screening and sorting to get to specific candidates more quickly. By efficient, we mean parsing technology that filtered résumés using specific, predetermined criteria. (Often, résumés without exact wording would be tossed. A common workaround for candidates was including white-on-white text that listed keywords that may be important to companies, thereby tricking the system into keeping their résumés.) Increased ATS functionality also allowed recruiters to trace an applicant's path through the different stages of the interview and hiring process.

By 2000, there were 40,000 commercial employment websites. By 2002, there were dozens of ATS options.[6] Countless other types of recruitment software have continued to flood the market, including candidate relationship management (CRM), interviewing programs, reference checking, human capital management, onboarding, and prehire candidate testing.

Today, the average employer uses five different recruitment tools per open job, and job seekers use an average of 16 resources in their job search.[7] All of these options were meant to make searching and hiring more efficient and foolproof, but is it working?

No. Because no one is actually addressing the problem.

A World of Band-Aids

Everyone thinks they know the problem. Or more precisely, people contribute their recruitment woes to a handful of different ones.

At the top of the list is speed. And it's true that one of the biggest talent challenges is the speed with which recruitment needs to be deployed or redeployed. In the world of tech alone, matching the right talent from among a scarce population of engineers fast enough to build companies while their ideas are still cutting edge is a problem. In 2021, Facebook announced it needed to hire 10,000 engineers within five years to help create its metaverse. Amazon needed to hire 40,000 corporate employees and 100,000 nonseasonal fulfillment workers. Invenergy, a developer and operator of sustainable power generation projects, said it needed to double in size over the next 12 months to keep up with new demands for its technology solutions. Oracle listed over 11,000 job openings, a huge percentage of which were developer positions. Microsoft needed 23,500 new workers to push its cloud-based workstation service over the finish line.[8]

Sectors outside of tech—health care, leisure and hospitality, education, construction, etc.—are experiencing the same type of rapid employment needs. Of course, many industries were disproportionately affected by the Covid-19 pandemic and are still playing catch up.

Whatever led to the substantial declines in output and employment, the fact remains that millions of jobs need to be filled. And fast.

Inopportunely, recruitment is a historically slow process. Industry reports reveal the average time to hire—which measures the speed at which a candidate is processed, assessed, interviewed, and accepted for a job—is 41 days (to get a bit more granular, engineering is slowest at 49 days and administrative is quickest at 33). And that metric doesn't include the time it takes to source the candidate, which the average recruiter estimates takes up nearly one-third of their work week (or, 13 hours) for a single role. What's more, top prospects are off the market in 10 days.[9]

So in the name of efficiency, employers implement a number of tools that automate, source, organize, communicate, assess, track, schedule, analyze, and facilitate the process. More tools! Faster tools! A tool for the tool! Many end up creating a recruiting assembly line and are drowning in tool chaos. But it's worth it to them because they presume if they could just do everything more quickly, they'll get to the candidate sooner and win in a tight employment market.

This brings us to another huge sticking point in recruitment: shortage of talent. As of 2022, there were 6 million people classified as unemployed in the United States and 11.5 million job openings. But it's an issue of quality as much as quantity. A reported 75% of global companies with 250+ employees said they struggled with a lack of qualified candidates. By comparison, 72% of medium (50–250 employees), 64% of small (10–49 employees), and 63% of micro (less than 10 employees) businesses reported the same issue.[10]

Promises have been made to solve these problems. Job boards will do it through aggregation. ATS systems will do it through organization. Automated Video Interviews (AVI) will do it through interpretation. Online assessments will do it through competency calculation. Work simulations will do it through observation.

Each phase of the process has an available tool or five, yet companies' unprecedented struggle to recruit and retain top talent is as significant as ever. We believe that instead of helping with comprehensibility, the profusion of tools has actually made it more narrow. The big picture is too hard to see. And getting lost in the details is what's most important of all: figuring out whether a person and company are the right fit for each other.

Intention, Not Reaction

When we started our company, we entered a crowded market that touted a bunch of "solutions." There was no shortage of tasks these tools tackled, workflows they streamlined, or information they gathered. They seemed to meet every need a recruiter could have. But as we peeled the layers back and studied all the things these tools did, we realized that what they *didn't* do was the problem.

The first was that none addressed what we saw as the underlying issue: sourcing terrific talent. No amount of screening software will help employers find the right talent if those candidates aren't in the mix to begin with. It puts the whole "shortage of talent" thing in a new light. Back in the day when we used Yahoo! to search the web and couldn't find what we wanted, it wasn't due to a shortage of websites. It was because the tool we were using wasn't capable of deciphering what we were actually looking for.

The second was the absence of humanity. There were tons of different tools that served tons of different functions. Yet we not only noticed what the technology did, but what it took away: person-to-person interaction, human intuition, conversation, connection. In a field as personal as recruitment, it was shocking to us that touch points weren't integral pieces baked right into these strategies.

To us, recruitment is about people—their lives, their dreams, their next steps. People are looking for jobs that fit their skill sets, a job with a company that aligns with their personality and lifestyle, and an employer that both appreciates who they are and sees their potential. There's a commercial component to it, of course. This is how they make money; this is their professional life. But it's intrinsically personal. It's a part of their soul, it's who they are.

Technology can aid the process in strategic and important ways, but there are limits to what we can expect it to solve. Consider this: Many of us at one point or another have decided we need a better organization system. Ultimately, we deem our notebooks to be the problem. We need new ones. If we get new notebooks, it will fix everything and all will be well. But it never is. And that's the story of a lot of technology in this space; generally, they provide really narrow solutions that lean into *a* problem, not *the* problem. Without addressing the structural damage, if you will, all that's built upon it will teeter. And no amount of software or gadgetry or notebooks will fix it.

That's where we found ourselves after discovering the two gaping holes in the current market. And our mission became clear: focus on the foundation. In the literal sense, this meant building a tool that started with sourcing, the proverbial ground floor of the great recruitment high-rise. In the figurative sense, this meant staying rooted in the knowledge of who all this was for.

5

The Future of Work

In the 1980s, data science revolutionized the credit market through default probability. Someone would apply for a credit card or loan, and automatic default probability calculations based on sociodemographic data determined the likelihood that a borrower wouldn't be able to make scheduled repayments. As such, credit offerings were based on whether the applicant had a high or low default probability. Since banks earned income by managing risk, this was considered a logical strategy.

But in the early 1990s, two management consultants, Richard Fairbank and Nigel Morris, started to poke holes. They saw that everybody in America had the same terms, and half of America couldn't qualify. They discovered that large banks were charging everyone a 19.8% annual percentage rate for their cards and justifying the high cost by pointing to the significant number of card borrowers who defaulted on their debt. As they questioned bankers further, they learned that banks made little effort to explore customers' creditworthiness. Banks had a standard for extending credit, preferring people who had lived in their homes for four years and had never been delinquent on their payments. They seemed to make no attempt to identify people who had been delinquent but might still be creditworthy.

Fairbank and Morris saw an opportunity for bank profitability using metrics other than just default probability. They recommended a radical idea: rebuild the credit-predictive system. In order to do that, they would need to access tons of data to model profitability. Every major bank they pitched said no. The idea of experimenting with financial products, especially credit cards, was heretical. Plus, banks didn't have that kind of raw data; the only data points they had were based on the terms they actually offered in the past and the sort of customer who was actually offered credit after being deemed worthy against the existing model. But Fairbank and Morris were undeterred. They believed that information technology was powerful enough to do sophisticated predictive modeling and change one-size-fits-all marketing into mass-customized solutions for consumers.

They finally garnered the interest of a small Virginia-based bank, Signet Bank. The bank's management became convinced that modeling profitability, not just default probability, was the right strategy. They knew that a small proportion of customers actually accounted for *more than* 100% of a bank's profit from credit card operations, the rest were breaking even or losing money. If they could model profitability, they could make better offers to the best customers and "skim the cream" off profitable credit accounts larger banks wouldn't offer.

It took five years to acquire the appropriate data. They started by conducting experiments where different terms were offered at random to different customers. The number of bad accounts soared, as you might expect, and Signet went from an industry-leading "charge-off" rate (2.9% of balances went unpaid) to almost 6% charge-offs. But it was imperative data and they believed the value was sufficient enough to justify the investment.[1]

Fairbank and Morris collected the standard data like sociodemographic backgrounds and their respective profitability, but also aggregated behavioral data—which had never been done before—such as customers' individual (anonymized) transactions and seasonal spending, and then incorporated the default probability. They slowly built predictive models, then evaluated and deployed them. When a customer called looking for a better offer, data-driven models calculated the potential profitability of various possible actions (different offers, including the status quo) and the representative's computer presented the best offers to make. Fairbank and Morris proved what they had presumed to be true: A demographically targeted approach, with customized terms, would generate a more efficient return.

Signet started a credit division using this new, data-driven methodology and a breakthrough product offer emerged: the credit card balance transfer. It became so popular and profitable that the division spun off from Signet and became Capital One. Fairbanks and Morris became Chairman and CEO and President and COO, and it grew to be one of the largest credit card issuers in the industry with one of the lowest charge-off rates.

To us, the implication is clear: Those with bigger data assets have an important strategic advantage over their smaller competitors. That said, it's not what you've got, it's how you use it.

Data Is as Data Does

Today, successful companies utilize data in significant ways. Many times it's used to determine the best way to approach new products or services. One way that Apple, for example, uses data is for application design; by studying how people use apps in real life, they alter future designs to fit with customer tendencies. Netflix analyzes "plays," ratings, and searches to determine what types of original programming should be developed; when numbers indicated Adam Sandler no longer had the same draw he once did in the US and UK markets, Netflix green-lighted four new films with the actor, based on knowledge that his previous work had been successful in Latin America. Procter & Gamble aggregates and filters external data, like comments and news mentions, on P&G's products and brands, allowing them to react as market developments occur; Tide Cleaners, a branded dry cleaning franchise from P&G, was developed after consumer insights about the deficits of the existing dry cleaning industry.[2]

Other times data is used to customize user experience. Starbucks utilizes data on customers' request inclinations and purchasing behavior to send out tailored offers. McDonald's uses real-time variables like weather, time of day, and popular items in specific locations to automatically change the digital menu boards in the drive-thru. Amazon analyzes customers' purchasing patterns, items in the shopping cart or wish list, and prior product reviews to produce targeted suggestions. Spotify studies raw audio data like a song's BPM, musical key, and loudness to classify songs based on music type and optimize its recommendation engine.[3]

Data can also be used to improve processes. UberEats wants to deliver food while it's still warm so it collects data around how much time it usually takes to prepare a certain meal in order to pinpoint the exact time the delivery person should come and pick up. It also employs meteorologists who use data to help predict what the weather will be like and how it will affect delivery. As many other companies do, Deloitte uses data to determine bottlenecks in productivity among staff. When it found its customer support team was spending an inordinate amount of time answering the same customer queries again and again, they created an FAQ section on their website to answer those repeat questions. The US Women's Soccer Team uses heart rate sensors and GPS systems to monitor player performance. Devices placed in their sports bras measure metrics like top speed, total distance run, high-intensity bursts, and time spent in specific areas of the field. Coaches use this data to assess the health and capabilities of their players and adjust game plans for particular matches; players use it to inform their recovery and training.[4]

These use cases are just the tip of the iceberg. Data can shed light on almost every aspect of an organization or industry and play a crucial role in providing value to both companies and consumers. And with how accessible all of this information has become, it's no wonder data crunching has become the cornerstone that it has.

The recruitment industry is no different; data is increasingly being used in every part of the funnel: First, basic applications like candidate qualifications, company criteria, and open role info are used to source; second, interest rate (as in, what percentage of people respond saying they're interested), how different open roles are performing, and source-to-hire ratios are used to optimize the process; and third, diversity and adverse impact metrics are used to negate bias. But there's also a wider use of data that, when collected and interpreted appropriately, can provide companies with invaluable insights into the hiring landscape as a whole, their own brand perception, and a candidate's experience with their recruitment process.

We all know that when people have a less-than-ideal experience with a company—its product, its customer service, its hiring process—they talk. In fact, the White House Office of Consumer Affairs released an array of statistics that showed the dissemination of complaints: A dissatisfied customer will tell between 9–15 people about their experience; negative interactions with a business are spread to twice as many people as positive ones; and it takes 12 positive experiences to make up for a single bad experience.[5]

Virgin Media learned this lesson the hard way when their first-ever "Rejected Candidate Survey" uncovered that 18% of their candidates were customers, and 33% of them had such an atrocious recruitment experience—much of which revolved around the interview process—that they switched to a competitor. The revenue lost from these former customers was estimated to be around $5 million, the same amount they had spent on hiring. What's more, Virgin's Net Promoter Scores (NPS), which measures how likely someone is to recommend a business, showed that two-thirds of rejected candidates were "detractors," meaning they likely wouldn't recommend Virgin to others.[6]

Based on these insights, the HR manager knew he had to make some changes to Virgin's hiring process. His motivation was threefold: candidates deserved better, the challenge of improving the candidate experience was something his recruiting team could find purpose in and draw meaning from, and it could improve the company's bottom line. He and his team embarked on the daunting task of retraining hundreds of employees on the benefits of providing a high standard of service, to not only their customers but also job candidates who were potential customers. They then created a "gold standard" interview program for their 450 hiring managers, and introduced incentives for those who offered the best candidate experience. The results exceeded expectations, particularly notable being Virgin's NPS moved from an overall −29 to +12.[7]

At Teamable, we love using data to gain insightful information that can help improve our client's processes. One company we work with is a popular consumer app, and its hiring process is huge—something like 10 steps, including a take-home assessment. The feedback we repeatedly heard from candidates was that the process was far too long. On Glassdoor, candidates were passionate about the product but didn't love the experience, particularly the take-home assignment. We pushed our clients to at least pay candidates for doing the take-home work, but they wanted to be fair to current employees and others who had previously done it without getting paid. As a result, some of their best candidates dropped out of the process.

Another client of ours in the financial sector found their perfect match in a candidate; she was exactly what they wanted. The candidate wasn't really considering making a move at the time, but the role and company were attractive to her—so much so that she was willing to move across the country to take it. But it all got derailed when she failed the coding assessment. The real shame was that the test measured for skills that weren't used in the day-to-day function of the job; it was a useless hoop candidates had to jump through that wasn't applicable to the role. And really, people who tended to score well on the skills test did so because they had a different skill set, which meant they were weaker in the areas the company really wanted the candidate to have. So not only was the assessment not a relevant measure of job performance, it actually skewed the candidates towards people our client didn't even want to hire.

Similarly, we have a customer that works in the autonomous vehicle space. They ultimately passed on over 320 candidates in one year because they "did not meet the skills bar." Yet by tracking the candidates' eventual whereabouts, we saw they went on to get jobs at Amazon, Google, Meta (Facebook), and Microsoft. The fact that those candidates were able to perform well at companies of equal caliber indicated to us there was a problem in our clients' hiring process.

By seeing where candidates drop off, as in the case of the laborious take-home assessment, or tracking where rejected or dropped candidates end up, we're able to see cracks in clients' hiring processes and encourage them to reexamine specific pieces of it. Comprehensive insights can lead to meaningful change for companies and candidates alike, and can only be leveraged by aggregating and analyzing relevant data to find patterns and trends that inform smarter hiring decisions.

Software Eats Recruiting

We launched our company knowing the way we chose to use data would separate us from our competitors in two crucial ways. Most obviously, the more quality data we had on potential candidates (keyword here is quality), the better our ability to ensure a right fit between prospect and client.

For the last two decades, the mecca for candidate sourcing has been LinkedIn because recruiters have access to millions of professional profiles that can be sorted by specific titles, qualifications, and/ or keywords. But we saw a gap. Basic search functionality is . . . basic. Anyone could, in theory, look through LinkedIn and find suitable matches at relatively basic levels. We were more interested in finding the exceptional than the suitable, and believed that was only possible if we accessed higher-quality data and then used it creatively to determine nuanced information.

For outbound recruiting, our sourcing software allows us to scour data from all corners of the internet. Anything clients ask for in a candidate, we can find. But we wholeheartedly believe that companies don't want someone to spit out exactly what they ask for. Plenty of services could do that. Companies want someone to understand what they actually want, Google-style, and solve the problems that exist between where they are and where they want to be. For us, this means getting around deficiencies of the job post and the résumé so that we can make better matches.

Early on, a client of ours was a cool start-up that wanted to hire for their employee payroll product, and it would have been pretty easy to find a match by going off the straightforward job description. But the conversation our recruiter had with the client prior to sourcing provided some pertinent information. First, the way the client spoke about running payroll was distinct. Passionate, excitable, focused around the newest technology. Second, the client referenced his work as a mentor for the Future Business Leaders of America (FBLA) multiple times.

Our perceptive recruiter drew the following assumptions: The client would react favorably to someone who was as stimulated as he is by financial products, and the client values commitment and leadership, as indicated by the subject of his mentoring work.

Those were insights only a human recruiter could have gathered. And then using them as data points, that recruiter got creative with how those traits might present in a candidate. Maybe someone new to the field, say no more than five years at a relevant company, would share the client's zest (not an age thing, but about getting to them before their enthusiasm waned); maybe a person whose thesis covered the most innovative niche technology within the financial sector would be as enthusiastic about the tech as the client; maybe someone who's an Eagle Scout would indicate high levels of commitment; maybe someone who'd been heavily involved in student government in college showed superior leadership skills. You get it.

Treating humans as data points can be positive or negative— boiling them down to just a few key numbers is a huge miss. But look at DNA. If your DNA was turned into computer code, it would have 75 million lines! You can learn so much about someone by examining that data. Even more so when it's coupled with their actions and what they'd done with that DNA. Recruiting is the same. We can learn so much about people, but only if we approach it the right way.

It's not what you've got, it's how you use it, remember? We didn't want to use data to just find someone who could talk about marketing, we wanted to find someone who talked about marketing in the *right* way. We could have just found a "leader" by searching for people who used that keyword, but we wanted to find someone whose initiative was proven and prevalent. Merging human creativity and data, we focused on unconventional touch points, building similarity engines, and perfecting our search.

The less obvious, yet equally important, way we intended to use data was to automate outreach. If sourcing is the proactive searching for qualified job candidates, outreach is making contact with that candidate about a role. It's usually done in the form of email messages that appeal to individuals based on their skills or background. Further, if the prospect is interested, outreach also includes getting them to the next phase of the hiring process, typically an interview.

The thought of automating these tasks would cause any self-respecting recipient to squirm. And with good reason. Most of us associate it with the generic messages we've all received from a recruiter. One that didn't include any personal details, aside from our autofilled name, nor a concrete reason why we'd be a good fit, which we wouldn't because the role couldn't have been more ill-fitting if it tried. (If you're an experienced engineer of 15 years getting a junior software engineer outreach, that's just insulting.) What's more, if it turns out we are indeed interested, we're tasked with following a link to the interviewer's availability and scheduling it ourselves.

We didn't want to automate outreach so a recruiter could blast out impersonal and/or irrelevant mass emails to 1,000 people at a time. Nor did we want to condone a scheduling process where people felt like they were in a one-sided negotiation over whose schedule was more important to work around. We wanted to automate outreach to make the entire experience more human. Hear us out.

A best-case scenario in the standard world of outbound recruiting is: a recruiter looks at a profile, finds an associated email, and writes the prospect a nice note about something they saw on their profile so they know the sender isn't a robot. The recruiter does that all day long. Then a few days later, they go back in and reply to all their previous emails, bumping them up to say, "Just touching base. I know things get lost in inboxes. I'd love to talk." They do that repetitive work despite the massive amount of time it takes.

For argument's sake, let's say they have nothing but time. Humans are historically bad at these types of tasks. How many times have you entered an email address incorrectly? Or misspelled a name that you clearly knew how to spell? Or struggled with time management and forgot to do things like follow-up? Humans are fallible. We're busy, distractible, and flawed.

Automating these outreach functions eliminated human error and removed the tedious tasks that fill a recruiter's day. But at the same time, we knew we couldn't rely solely on automation; doing so would go against the impersonality that we're so adamantly against, not to mention we knew leaving everything up to technology wasn't foolproof either (Microsoft's conversational bot that offended nearly everyone in less than 24 hours comes to mind). The solution was to strategically blend the power of tech with the power of humans, splitting the automation between what robots and humans were each best at.

For example, let's say the name on your LinkedIn profile reads john smith. It isn't capitalized (it was a style choice). If you get an email from a recruiter that opens with "Hi john," it's likely a robot. A human would have capitalized it. That's annoying and doesn't give the best first impression, but it's not the worst.

Now imagine if you were born Robert and transitioned. Your feelings would be hurt (and you'd form a negative impression of the company that's recruiting you) if automation just pulled your old name out and used it. But if a human looks at it, they can see that the recommendations people have written on your LinkedIn show a switch from one name to another over time. The name in the URL may be different from the name under the photo. The human can put the pieces together to understand the timeline in order to choose the correct name. And when you receive an outreach later that day where the recruiter uses your preferred name, it feels nice. Personal. It's a sign of kindness, not a shortcut.

The email may have been automated but the personalization was all human; it took an easy-to-automate task but paired it with the oversight of a real person. We built an entire outreach engine under that premise. To execute it, our team manually did the process our product now automates, catching over and over and over again the idiosyncratic details of candidates to ensure communication was done in the most respectful, relevant, and individualized way. We learned from each use case and automated our process bit by bit to ensure we never sacrificed quality.

It's a thread we've kept all the way through the growth of our company. Do everything by hand, exposing human creativity at each stage in order to learn from it and automate it effectively, but always keep a team in the loop.

The Human Touch

Connectivity is something we feel is lacking in recruitment today. Not connecting people to jobs or companies to candidates, although that too, but connecting with all parties on a personal level. Both candidates and companies' representatives deserve to be treated as people, not prospects; it's the only way to truly ascertain what they want and need and effectively help them find it.

Underpinning that motivation is the simple truth that what people are looking for is always changing. We live in a fast-paced world and our professional and personal lives are continuously impacted by everything from technological advances to market shifts, environmental conditions to political unrest, social justice standards to global pandemics. These consequential factors directly influence our priorities, choices, demands, and expectations, and understandably so.

For example, the COVID-19 pandemic was inarguably the single most significant driver of rapid change for businesses in recent history. It forced them to rethink every element of their day-to-day operations as supply chains were interrupted, demand for products and services declined, brick-and-mortar stores faced government-mandated closures, and in-office work was relegated to at-home. For their part, many employees found themselves in one of two camps: they still had a job but it looked different in every discernible way, or they no longer had a job.

A true catalyst, the pandemic created short-term disruptions and provoked long-term changes in how the world lives and does business. For companies, prescribed approaches and standardized solutions would no longer cut it. For employees, Ping-Pong tables and weekly happy hours would no longer suffice. For job seekers, promises of vision benefits and a corner office would no longer be enough. What mattered to them had fundamentally changed, and it was our job to have a steady pulse on it.

In the midst of Covid, our data showed that both men and women mentioned child care as a barrier to their interviewing for a new job. It impacted women at about three times the rate, but both genders had to reschedule interviews because of child care shutdowns—or to decline an opportunity to pursue a role because they needed to be home with their kids who couldn't attend day care because of Covid or who were attending virtual school.

We noticed that, in 2020, customers began mentioning their open roles were remote at 2.5 times the rate they did the year before. Side-note: These were campaigns that proactively mentioned the work-from-home status. Many others were remote but may only be listed as such in the linked job description or discussed in the interview. In those cases, candidates often replied to inquire if it was remote, as they were not open to returning to an office in any capacity.

We saw a huge shift to cities like New York, Austin, and Miami for founders and angel investors; they didn't feel as tied to San Francisco to find strong talent anymore. And candidates were also moving, but even more broadly than founders. Customers sourced seven times more engineering candidates in Colorado in 2022 than 2019, and there was ten times the demand for engineering candidates in Alaska over that same time period. Talented engineers were now able to relocate to places that made them happier employees, and customers were no longer limited by an expensive physical location to conduct their hunt for talent.

Four times as many people talked about cost of living influencing their reasons for turning down job opportunities in certain locations and/or for wanting to work remotely because of a move to a cheaper location. There's been a 25,000% increase—which is difficult to even write because it's so ridiculous—of people who respond saying they have moved or intend to move out of California/the Bay Area.

Five times as many candidates said they were seeking more balance in their lives, typically work/life balance; they were moving away from jobs that are all-consuming. We had never seen someone respond by mentioning burnout, and then people mentioned it quite freely, almost always in that they had made a change because of the burnout they had experienced in their previous role.

There was a huge uptick of candidates who discussed the importance of a company's stance on social issues—LGBTQ initiatives, mental health resources, or even a company's location in a state that had limited access to reproductive care—as a tipping point in their decision to proceed or not.

These types of insights are crucial for companies to comprehend where the candidates are, figuratively speaking, and assess whether and how they could meet them there. It's essentially a commitment to think holistically about candidates. Where were they before and why did they leave? What are their core motivations? What are they about? You're hiring for the whole person, so it's important to understand who they are, not just whether or not they meet qualifications.

One of our recruiters was working on a Senior Fullstack Engineer campaign for a stealth mode, eight-person start-up. A candidate responded with interest, and on paper was an absolute home run; he checked all the boxes the Head of Engineering was looking for. A great 30-minute conversation confirmed the recruiters' thoughts about the candidate being a good fit. Only one small thing: even though the candidate's LinkedIn profile indicated that he had been working at a well-known e-learning company for the past five years, it turned out he had left the company to join a start-up just eight weeks prior to the call. He went into detail about how the company was sold to him during the interview process, and how the polar opposite was the case the moment he began working there. The situation the candidate described sounded like a nightmare, and our recruiter understood why he had wanted to leave, and with urgency.

The problem was, the client was explicit about the fact that they wouldn't entertain any candidate who was a job hopper—typically someone who has work stints of one year or less. Under no circumstances would they be interested in someone willing to leave a company after just eight weeks.

But our recruiter felt strongly that the candidate was ideal, and after hearing his story, was hell-bent on helping him get out of a bad situation. When the recruiter contacted the client's Head of Engineering to tell them about the conversation, they were very hesitant. But the recruiter pushed them to speak, citing the candidate's desire to work in a start-up environment, his solid tenure at every company he'd previously worked for, and his ample experience with the appropriate technologies.

The Head of Engineering agreed to have an exploratory call. The candidate was indeed perfect, and was hired two weeks later.

Another of our recruiters was working with a B2B2C client that was hiring software engineering managers. There was a candidate who didn't have a strong résumé, but the recruiter felt she was a strong prospect based on initial screening. She was articulate; how she described her previous work was impressive. She had discernment; her questions about the role and the company were intelligent and comprehensive. She had similar values as the client; her volunteer work aligned with the important community initiatives the company supported.

The recruiter wrote a summary of the interaction with the candidate, along with a caveat that the résumé didn't truly capture her skillset. After some convincing, the hiring manager finally relented, and the candidate turned out to be a tremendous asset to the organization.

Human intuition can be so underrated.

Some of our clients have their own in-house recruiters, and we're endlessly fascinated by how they approach candidate sourcing using our product and what the results are. Erika is a recruiter at software company Databricks, and extremely intentional with her searching. Instead of just relying on keywords, she studies profiles and takes all kinds of data points into consideration. When she finds someone who she thinks may be a good fit, she asks for 15 minutes of their time. She wants to speak with them and find out what's happening in their lives. Are they happy where they are? Why or why not? If open to a change, what types of things are important, both professionally and personally? It's the exact opposite of a sales pitch; it's learning about people and digging into the root of what drives them. In doing so, Ericka drills down on who would be excited about working at Databricks and excel while there. As a result, the rate at which candidates respond to her outreach saying they're interested in speaking is sometimes 50% higher than the rest of her team. Furthermore, the candidates she interviews turn into hires at a much greater rate, likely because of the relationships she's built.

For as individualized as her approach is, her volume is incredibly high. She's the classic example of someone who understands that teams are made up of real people who have career goals and personal lives and backgrounds that can never be summed up on a one-page résumé or LinkedIn profile. So Ericka dissected those conversations and looked at what they really meant. What was consistent about the people with whom she was seeing success? She set aside any assumptions she'd had about what backgrounds she should target and instead looked at what had worked in reality. She invested time into identifying those complex motivations. And once she understood them, she was able to scale it by treating it as actionable data. She found candidates who matched what she'd found out to be true indicators of success, and she targeted them, sourcing at a pace no one else could keep up with. Over the past year, Ericka has been responsible for over a quarter of the entire company's sourcing on our platform, and she's still in first place when it comes to the rate at which candidates interview and are hired.

Adam from Coinbase is another of our favorite recruiter examples. He finds people who he knows are perfect fits and targets them. If they're not interested, he sets up a follow-up to go out a full year later. This is a very successful tactic and ultimately why his hired rate is so high. He finds people who are perfect for the company—people who, if they interviewed, would very likely get hired—and he makes sure to catch them later on when they're interested in making a move. And it works. He's hired 5% more people than the rest of Coinbase recruiters put together.

These instances were a result of conversations and intentionally connecting with who people were and what they wanted. Taking the time to understand the current factors that influence people's decisions ensures everyone can be on the same page and truly get their needs met. It makes for better hires and, in the long run, better company culture.

Tech + Data + People

At Teamable, our goal is to reinvent how recruitment works entirely. It will not be by running a recruiting firm full of "better recruiters" who just learn how to do the work better than everyone else. That idea is hubristic at best; there are lots of smart people doing this work. What we add is that we are recruiters who are also technologists. We see a future where recruiting and technology come together to do something new. So, it's not exactly like anything else that exists.

We are an AI company. And because the definition of AI is when machines carry out the tasks a human normally does, we are simply the AI company for recruiting.

We displace lots of technologies that were built for recruiters—but not *by* recruiters—and so they miss the understanding that comes with doing the job. We have data products that push the boundaries of what's possible with person data. Our workflow products take manual work that recruiters do repeatedly, by hand, with software. Our search and matchmaking products give people an excellent way to see who matches a role, which they can tune as they browse profiles. It has to be interactive in this way, because that's how people build intuition around a search. An underappreciated fact is that, as much as Google learns what we like and delivers great search results, we also learn what Google likes. We learn how to make searches better. Finding talent is like that. We're building Google for recruiting. But we also change what it takes to do all of that—which is a multiple of recruiters, not recruiter tools. We care about changing what recruiting software means, but that's not the full story. We shake up how companies think about the conjoined pair of recruiting software and labor.

Humans can't comb through profiles to find the important features. AI misses nuanced things that make someone a viable option. Full automation wouldn't find these outliers without a human crafting a search that finds those criteria. Humans don't have the time or bandwidth for tedious, unmeaningful work. AI can't naturally spot the idiosyncratic details that matter in outreach. Technology needs to save workers from tedious, unfulfilling work, but it's not enough to just add AI.

There needs to be a solution that bridges the gap. There needs to be machine learning coupled with clever product parameters. There needs to be lots of good data, clearly defined problems, careful decision making about what and how to automate, and great software experiences around these constraints. There needs to be a combination of data-based certainty, scalability, and the seamless process of a tech solution with a human touch. There needs to be enterprise soft-ware that moves beyond "management" and delivers technology solutions that actually get the work done. There needs to be a complete end-to-end recruiting platform designed to put people first, always.

And now there is.

III

Rethink What It Could Mean

6

The Culture Crutch

On average, Americans spend 90,000 hours at work over a lifetime.[1] That's a *huge* chunk of our lives, and only trumped by the number of hours we spend sleeping. It's no wonder then that people want to feel happy and fulfilled at work. Not only do we spend more than one-third of our waking hours on the job, but we all know how jobs have a way of bleeding into every aspect of our life, significantly impacting its overall quality. Who wants to spend a third of their life doing something they find meaningless?

A recent study by PwC showed that meaning and fulfillment at work is the new standard employees expect of their work experience, and one that companies need to embrace if they want to cultivate the best workforce. But sadly, when thousands of employees were asked if they felt fulfilled at work, 49% of them answered no. Yet when those same people were asked whether or not they felt it was *possible* to be fulfilled at work, 96% said yes.[2]

When recruiters and candidates engage, this is the root of the conversation. People looking for their next play are looking for something they want to do. Of course, some just have a goal in mind, but for most work is just as much about the journey as the destination. They want something that feels good day in and day out. They are looking for fulfillment.

Recruiters are no different. Ask any recruiter, and they love the satisfaction of helping someone find their next new thing. It is a growth experience for candidates. It matters to them. And companies feel it too. The feeling of adding a great person to the team is exhilarating, and it's what helps everyone get better. Companies grow through their people, and recruiters are key representatives of the company. They represent their teams to new teammates, and so they need to feel empowered and free to do the important work of engaging with people. They need to be ready to have great conversations about perks, compensation, career trajectory and company culture, but they also need to take the time to figure out what's best for everyone. What is going to be most fulfilling all around.

The clear separation between people knowing it's possible yet being unable to achieve it is distressing at best. And it raises the question: With today's companies throwing everything they can—competitive salaries, robust benefits, impressive perks, flex options—to hire and retain top talent, how can there be such a prevalent lack of fulfillment?

Because those who think they can provide fulfillment through extrinsic motivation are missing a fundamental understanding of what fulfillment is all about.

There's a saying in the ad world: Don't tell me how good you make it, tell me how good it makes me when I use it. Think about that. When a customer buys your product, they're not buying your product. They're buying an imagined future. They're buying a promise of what life will be like once they've made their purchase. And once they do, your job is done, right? You made the sale. But will your product live up to its promise of improving their life?

Too often, company culture works the same way. Candidates are lured by the promise of how much better their lives will be once they're hired, and how could they not, what with all the bells and whistles thrown at them. They're sold on a perception, an illusion, a hope that this job, this team, this work environment offers them what's missing all along—the professional contentment that's evaded them thus far has finally arrived. But what happens afterwards, once they're in the trenches of the job? They quickly realize that 95% of their time is spent doing work, and only 5% of their time is spent playing Ping-Pong while drinking a beer. Toys lose their charm, the fluff wears off, and the work matters. They think back to what got them excited about the job in the first place. Things have to be as advertised, and the work needs to tie to a common goal. The key parts of what makes a team work well together, the glue of what we're all in it for, needs to be there.

So, is the 5% of time people spend with cool perks exciting and appreciated? Yes. Is the 95% far more important? Unequivocally so. And to fill your company with the people who will thrive in the 95% requires one thing: the realization that your company culture is about why you all do this. It's about why people joined in the first place. If people joined for the perks, your culture is about Ping-Pong tables. But if people joined for what the team accomplishes together, then it's about the why, and the mission, and that's far more likely to be an amazing experience that leads to a remarkable outcome.

The Culture Deck

For over two decades, Netflix has been one of the most sought-after places to work. Originally a DVD rental business with only 30 employees in 1998, technologists and creatives applied in droves over the years as Netflix transitioned into an online streaming service, and later, a production company. Fusing the world of Silicon Valley and Hollywood together, Netflix was a trailblazer, a disruptor, and an absolute magnet for the millennial workforce.

The draw of its innovation aside, high salaries and Google-style office perks were undoubtedly appealing to applicants. But what really set Netflix apart came courtesy of its 128-page "Culture Deck" that was released to the public in 2009. CEO Reed Hastings and his colleagues created the simple PowerPoint presentation to explain its management philosophy, including how the company shaped its culture and motivated performance among its employees. It was originally posted as a pre-employment tool to dissuade incompatible people from applying, but here's what happened instead: It went viral (21 million views and counting) and caused a widespread HR frenzy at companies everywhere.

Netflix's methodology behind its corporate culture was radical. In a world where every company seemed to have the same rules and processes, Netflix did a U-turn. It seemingly had no rules. Its processes hinged on freedom and responsibility, believing that responsible people, whom they referred to as "fully formed adults," were not only worthy of freedom, but thrived on it. It was a team of people "loosely coupled and highly aligned." Accordingly, Netflix offered things no one else did at the time, including unlimited vacation days for salaried employees (its policy:"Take vacation"), uncapped expense accounts ("Act in Netflix's best interest"), an open-ended parental leave policy ("Take care of yourself and your baby"), and no micro-managing ("We pride ourselves on how few, not how many, decisions our senior managers make").[3] The company did not offer perks and instead just passed on that budget in the form of higher salaries. After all, some fully formed adults might not like the same perks as others.

This radical departure from the norm was bold insofar as it called out the individual as central to the company's way of thinking. It would be a group of people who didn't need a bunch of microman-agement (loosely coupled) but who could rally around common goals and solve problems together (highly aligned). The types of people who wanted to join Netflix would lean into this idea. The culture deck was a recruitment tool, an open manifesto for a way of doing things that celebrated individuals over a monoculture.

The entire premise of its loose approach was that high performers didn't require hand-holding; the higher the quality of the workforce, the less the need for rules. But what Netflix lacked in conventional structure, it made up for in expectations. There were behaviors and skills that it valued in employees—among them were honesty, good judgment, communication, curiosity, and courage—and those who demonstrated them would be hired and promoted. All intangibles that you wouldn't see on a résumé would come out in their hiring process. They recognized that someone's why, what drives them, and how they grow, is really a reflection of the sort of company employees wanted. Companies are at their best when full of capable, driven, growth-oriented individuals. So they had big hiring challenges—to attract these folks. But they had to make sure the company held that bar to match what its team signed up for.

Like many companies, Netflix had to hire well. Unlike many companies, it was quick to act if those hires didn't meet A-level performance standards. The company viewed its employees as members of a pro sports team—as opposed to a family—in which every player had to be a star performer or they'd be cut, so to speak. To ensure that superstars filled every position, Netflix vowed to cut smartly, saying that "adequate performance gets a generous severance package," generally a minimum of four months full pay. If employees didn't produce sustained A-level performance, despite "A for effort," they were let go. If someone was a "brilliant jerk," they were seen as detrimental to great teamwork and were let go. If someone didn't pass the "keeper test," in which managers asked themselves if they would fight hard to keep an employee at Netflix if they found out that employee was leaving for a similar job at a peer company, they were let go.[4]

This seemingly constant threat of being fired could be seen as cruel, heartless, and ruthless, but Netflix was focused on innovation and monumental growth. If one employee was performing worse than the rest, Netflix believed that employee would drag the others down with them if there were no consequences; if there was no retribution, then the top performers would begin to realize that they could also underperform and nothing bad would happen.

Companies like GE and Microsoft have had policies like this that are interpreted similarly; they would stack rank employees and let a fixed percentage of the lowest performers go every year. It led to a threatening feeling of dread among employees, and to cutthroat and anxious performance management. Gaming the review system was a priority to the team, and looking out for oneself was incentivized. It was more important than solving problems together. The team's feelings of one another, and getting stuff done together, wasn't as important as the stack ranking. Of course it would be that way. Many companies followed the lead of this sort of policy.

And although many examples of rigid performance management like this abound, Netflix is performance driven to the extreme—there are no fixed quotas. People who thrive, stay. That is the only requirement. And it was only Netflix that led with the culture outlined in its deck. It had to deliver this to its employees because they signed up to be at a company that is run like a pro sports team.

Netflix's approach to company culture was tough but in a way that was well received by employees. Following the release of its culture deck in 2009, its workforce of less than 2,000 steadily grew to over 7,000 by 2018. That same year, it was voted the best place to work in the world, beating the likes of Google, Facebook, Amazon, and Apple. Its employee turnover was only 11% a year, below the 13% annual average for tech companies. And it ranked first in Employee Net Promoter Score, with 71% of employees saying they would encourage their friends to become coworkers.[5]

But then in 2021, cracks began to show. That was the year Netflix aired *The Closer*, Dave Chapelle's stand-up comedy special. Critics were vocal with their disapproval over what they perceived as transphobic and homophobic comments, and hundreds of Netflix employees felt the same. And those employees took to the company's long-standing Open Q&A doc, an internal communication where employees could ask executives tough questions and expect good-faith responses: Where does Netflix draw the line between commentary and hate speech? Is there a clear distinction made between offensiveness and harmfulness to populations when evaluating what content to buy and air? If we can measure an appetite from members for transphobic and bigoted content, will we start partnering with dangerous celebrities, actors, and comedians in an effort to entertain the world?[6]

Days passed and the questions remained unanswered, which was odd because co-CEO Reed Hastings had a reputation for answering queries from any department within a couple days, no matter how critical or sensitive. Instead, an internal memo written by co-CEO Ted Sarandos was distributed to staff. In it, Netflix employees were advised that if they were offended by the streamer's "content breadth," they should quit. Additionally, Netflix made updates to its culture deck, inserting a section on artistic expression that echoed the internal memo: "If you'd find it hard to support our content breadth, Netflix may not be the best place for you."[7]

The company's response, or perceived lack of an appropriate one, undoubtedly struck a nerve. People did not feel heard. They were given a hard-line stance, much like the sort of stack ranking system of GE, or micromanagement at another company. The company didn't open a conversation among "fully formed adults" and instead babied a group of people who opted out of that very conversation—which is exactly what the company was going for in the first place. Employees and supporters protested outside Netflix's headquarters as a show of solidarity with the trans community. Its trans employee resource group staged a walkout. Some employees quit, some were fired, some filed unfair labor practice charges against Netflix. Some filmmakers and comedians spoke out against Netflix, and an executive producer of one of its shows announced she would no longer work with the streamer.

Even though Netflix remained staunch in its decision not to take Chapelle's special off the platform, Sarandos later acknowledged in an interview that he "screwed up that internal communication" and "should have led with a lot more humanity." But the damage had been done: company morale was at an all-time low, support from the LGBTQ community waned, subscriber rates fell, and Netflix's stock price slipped.[8]

It was a puzzling turn of events. On the one hand, the actions of Netflix seemed in stark contrast to the expectations it had set with its employees around honesty. Netflix placed a premium on honesty, expected it from employees and leadership alike, and explicitly mentioned it in the culture deck numerous times. "Honest Always" one slide said. "Radical Candor" read another. Everyone at Netflix was expected to lead with truth, quickly admit to mistakes, and openly give and accept feedback. It was upon this foundation of communication and trust that the team's effectiveness would be magnified. These aren't traits that companies can create for people, but they can be environments that give oxygen to them. Without it, trust and communication shatters, and a group of loosely coupled people also becomes loosely aligned. Reluctance to have these conversations within the team had consequences.

What's more, Hastings cowrote a book with author Erin Meyer called *No Rules Rules: Netflix and the Culture of Reinvention* in 2020. In it, they outlined Netflix's philosophy around people management. While some new gems surfaced, most of the book's content provided a more in-depth look at the slides published 10 years earlier. One of those main concepts was around radical candor and transparency, and the authors restated their value by saying, "The day you question giving candid feedback is the day you should leave Netflix" and "It's tantamount to being disloyal to the company if you fail to speak up when you disagree with a colleague or have feedback that would be helpful."[9]

So in the wake of *The Closer* controversy, what happened to the expectation that employees give candid feedback? What happened to the tenets of communication and honesty? What happened to the value placed upon courage, defined in its culture deck as "You question actions inconsistent with our values"?

On the other hand, Netflix had never made a secret of its inflexibility—perhaps a better word is *decisiveness*—when it came to accomplishing sustained success and what it would and would not tolerate from its employees on its way to doing so. Those high expectations were public knowledge, and while they revolved around employee performance and behavior, they were also indicative of its overall culture: demanding, strategic, and unyielding.

To Netflix's credit, it knew the buy-in was steep and wouldn't be for everyone. And that was perfectly fine. Netflix didn't want to settle on incompatible employees, not only because it would result in a less than ideal product and environment, but because the employees themselves deserved better. Its generous severance package seemed a testament to that. As in—you deserve to be 100% fired up about your work, you deserve to work for a company where you'll be fulfilled and happy, you deserve to be appreciated for the work you produce. If it's not here, we're going to set you free so you can go find it.

Over the years, the culture at Netflix prompted a lot of people to want to work there (it fielded 350,000 job applications in 2019 alone).[10] But when push came to shove in 2021, it turned out the disgruntled employees needed more than top-of-market pay, a lack of rules, and extravagant perks. They needed to feel seen, connected, heard, and respected. They needed their values to align with those of their employer. They needed to not only believe in the mission but the routes taken to get there. As for the non-disgruntled employees, it can be assumed that they didn't feel ostracized, that their values weren't threatened, and that they weren't uncomfortable with the actions of the company. It's not a debate over which of the two was right or wrong—it's just a clear indication that one was the right fit for the company and the other wasn't. But what is not up for debate is that some people left the company for the same reasons they joined it in the first place. That is the big culture miss.

The Perks of Being a Worker

There are so many ways that companies try to keep their employees happy. Most of us think immediately of the strategic use of perks, which aren't as new as many people might think. The American Express Company offered the first US corporate pension plan in 1875. In 1910, President Taft suggested that every worker should get two to three months of vacation (Americans are still waiting). In 1912, Chicago-based Montgomery Ward offered employer-sponsored life insurance. In 1919, activists forming the International Labor Organization called for 12 weeks of paid maternity leave and free prenatal care. In the 1930s, industrialist Henry Kaiser teamed up with surgeon Sidney Garfield to create the Permanente Health Plan, a prepaid medical plan for workers. By the late 1940s, benefits like these were a mainstay of labor negotiations. But during World War II, when the major problem of inflation prompted lawmakers to limit the maximum hourly wages a worker could receive, companies struggled to hire and keep talented workers without the appeal of a higher paycheck or raises. Business owners weren't happy, nor were employees. That's when companies started offering extra incentives that were "on the fringe" of cash wages.[11]

Back then, fringe benefits consisted of paid vacations, pensions, and the occasional company car. By 1980, those benefits expanded to things like meals and lodging, dependent care assistance, and parsonage allowances. The 1990s saw companies get even more creative, offering perks like club passes, employer-paid legal help, errand runners, and stock options. And today, well, we all know the state of things today.

For many, Google is top of mind when it comes to perks. Among other countless offerings are its nap pods for midday siestas, on-site medical staff, laundry services, and in the event of an employee's death, spouses receive 50% of their salary for 10 years, plus $1,000 a month per child. And the food! Google doesn't just offer free meals, it offers over 30 on-site cafes at its headquarters that serve everything from sushi to Indian food to fresh fruit smoothies. On the off-chance employees don't see anything they like, they can provide feedback and suggestions using an internal system called "Foodback."[12]

Many other tech companies have followed suit. Asana, the Silicon Valley software start-up, provides organic home-cooked meals twice a day, life coaching services, on-site yoga classes, monthly Uber stipends, and a $10,000 allowance for workspace furnishing (yes, you read that right); Salesforce takes team trips to Hawaii, covers commuter expenses, and reimburses eligible expenses related to adopting a child; Zynga, a gaming company, has relaxation lounges with arcades and gaming systems, a free artisanal coffee bar, snack kitchens, and a rooftop dog park.[13]

These kinds of externally motivated perks transformed the face of work and seemed to go a long way for morale. But they do not solve the root of what people want.

The problem with all these perks is that they are things that anyone can do. You can just buy them. You can copy them from other companies. They may sound creative, but they are the least possible creative thing a company can do. One reason Netflix's policy was so radical was because it had no perks resembling stunts. Perks like a ball pit in the office are like candy. It might look colorful and feel great for a minute, but it is not food. And of course in 2020, office perks became irrelevant. Everyone worked from home, and flexibility when it came to child care, when to be online and how we did work was front and center. Companies that relied on fancy campuses suffered because the benefits were literally inaccessible.

As times have changed, so have priorities. Today, for example, employees are more socially conscious. A recent report revealed that 83% of workers thought their employer wasn't doing enough to be more sustainable and tackle climate change; 65% said they would be more likely to work for a company with robust environmental policies.[14] People want to work for companies that positively contribute to society and the greater good, and as such, they hold their employers accountable for the choices they make and the impact those choices have on an individual, local, and global scale. In response, companies of all sorts and sizes have adopted standards of sustainability and social responsibility, as well as introduced employee benefits that align with them.

Companies like Coca-Cola and Ameritech offer such benefits as donation matching and time off to volunteer. Others like Clif Bar and Honest Tea have a bike to work program that pays employees for leaving the car in the garage. Timberland encourages employees to take part in the local food movement through its 1,200 square foot fruit and vegetable garden on the front lawn of its global headquarters. Vermont Energy Investment Corp provides sustainability budgets for their employees to try a new sustainability idea or take action on an existing problem.[15]

Nike and Apple, among many others, have pledged to "go green" by using environmentally friendly material in their products and renewable energy sources in their manufacturing. DHL upgraded its delivery trucks to hybrid vehicles, implemented a GoGreen initiative that streamlines logistical operations and directs trucks to take the shortest route, and has a program in place where it helps airports get ready for natural disasters. Patagonia donates 10% of its profits to environmental causes and groups, encourages consumers to return worn-out clothing so it can be recycled or repurposed (which is done in its clothing repair facility, the largest one of its kind in North America), and doesn't use any chemicals in its production processes.[16]

This isn't just for employee benefit, obviously. These are important actions in response to major, widespread problems. But the fact that companies are taking responsibility in the area that employees are requesting—well, it goes a long way for connectedness and value alignment. Plus, it's making a difference. As the importance of sustainability grows, accountability practices have become more widely adopted. According to the *Global Sustainable Investment Alliance* report in 2020, global sustainability investment had topped $35 trillion, up 15% from 2018, 68% since 2014, and tenfold since 2004.[17]

And finally (at least insofar as we're covering the topic), there's another thing employees progressively want from their employers: flexibility. We touched on it earlier, but it's worth reiterating that recent events—most notably, the pandemic—fundamentally changed what people were looking for and what they're willing to accept. For many, remote or hybrid work and flexible scheduling isn't a luxury but a necessity, and they expect their employers to meet them where they are.

According to the *Society for Human Resource Management (SHRM)*, nearly a third of workers have sought out a new job because their current workplace didn't offer flexible work opportunities; 80% (up from 75% in 2018) said that they would be more loyal to their employers if they had flexible work options; 52% of respondents tried to negotiate flexible work arrangements with their companies; more than 25% said they would take up to a 20% pay cut in exchange for a flexible work arrangement.[18]

The need is real, and companies are responding. As of 2022, companies like Hubspot, which had 10% of its workforce already working from home pre-pandemic, now let employees choose whether they want to work in-office, flex, or from home. Vistaprint has become a remote-first company, giving its 6,500 employees across 17 countries freedom and flexibility in the name of building a culture more conducive to enhancing physical and mental health. Twitter declared that employees would have the ability to "work from home forever" or "wherever you feel most productive and creative."[19]

Many companies are rising to the occasion and listening to their employees. One wonders though if the hoops companies are jumping through are all for naught. There will be no end to the tides of change that affect employees, thereby determining what they need from employers. It's not that employees don't deserve bells and whistles— they undoubtedly do—but will perks result in fulfillment at work?

Only if they're in the right role at the right company.

On the Hunt

Fulfillment. We all want it, chase it, and some even claim they've found it. But what is it really? A feeling? An objective state? An emotion? It depends on who you ask.

For some, fulfillment means pleasure and satisfaction. As reflected in today's popular acronyms like YOLO, there are people who take fulfillment to mean enjoying life; to go one further, that if it feels good, they should do it. This can range from racking up dopamine-boosting "likes" on social media, devouring a super-sized meal, or splurging on a new gadget. At work, it can mean partaking in free yoga classes at work, getting to fly in the company jet, or being granted "pawternity" leave. One could argue that recipients feel fulfilled in those instances, and they may. But it won't last. It can't. It's short-term elation packaged as a long-term remedy. These are pleasurable experiences and can give people a temporary boost, but it's not built upon anything substantial.

Others define fulfillment as the completion of a goal or a promise. It seems inherently linked to accomplishment—as in, we feel fulfilled after we've accomplished something. Stereotypical examples are making a certain amount of money, losing a certain amount of weight, or walking a certain amount of steps in a day. Specific work-related examples would be mastering a new system, meeting a sales quota, or answering all the emails in your inbox. The trouble is, the threshold and content of accomplishments that constitute fulfillment are wholly subjective. What's more, the achievements themselves have different magnitudes and can carry significantly more weight from one person to the next. Not to mention, it promotes a when-then mindset. *When* I finish these reports, *then* I'll be happy. *When* I make tenure, *then* I'll feel fulfilled. *When* I get a raise, *then* I'll feel worthy. It's a slippery slope as people keep switching their benchmarks when they either didn't reach a particular goal or still didn't feel fulfilled once they did. There's nothing wrong with evolving aspirations, but therein lies the downside to the mentality of accomplishment leading to fulfillment: it's conditional, not foundational.

To us, fulfillment doesn't mean momentary happiness or the accomplishment of something. It goes way deeper than that. We believe fulfillment is about engaging every part of yourself in pursuit (note: not achievement) of a goal; it's about doing work that you enjoy and that grows with you over time.

One of our favorite stories is that of Hamdi Ulukaya. In 2005, he left Turkey to study English in New York City. Even though he was happy he made the move, he was homesick—he missed his family, his farm, even his favorite foods. Nothing he found in New York even came close to the products his own dairy farm had made. When Hamdi took a friend up on an invite to travel upstate, he was unaware that not far away from his new, bustling urban life was a landscape that reminded him of all he'd left behind. He instantly fell in love. So he stayed.

Hamdi wasn't sure of his plan—get a job, maybe start a business? All he knew was that something drew him to that place. He knew he missed his old way of life, but he also considered the business world to be harsh and uncaring; in order for a few people to succeed, many others had to fail.

He saw it firsthand, even in his newly adopted small town. A local yogurt factory was being shuttered and the 55 employees who depended on the work to support their families were now tasked with breaking down the equipment while trying to figure out their next steps. After decades in operation, the global corporation that owned it was pulling out. It affirmed what Hamdi had always suspected: Someone in a glass tower had made a decision without considering how it would impact the people who had worked diligently to serve them.

A flier was circulated advertising the sale of the factory. Hamdi threw it in the trash. If the former owners who had obvious business acumen couldn't make the operation successful, how could he? He admittedly knew nothing about business or marketing or financing. But he knew how to make yogurt, and he wanted other people to experience what he knew was a better way of doing things. He couldn't shake the feeling that maybe he could make it work.

One of the factory's employees—a man who had devoted 20 years to the plant—gave him a tour. Before him, his father and grandfather had worked within the now-crumbling walls. Hamdi heard the same twinge of sadness that he carried himself. They shared the same dream. Something mattered to them, and they thought it could matter to others as well. If only they could figure out how to share their dream with other people.

So Hamdi bought the factory. And he hired four of the 55 factory employees, including the man who'd made such an impression on him during his tour. On their first day, they sat together and one of the new hires asked, "What do we do now?" Hamdi wasn't sure. Where should they even begin? So he announced they'd make a trip to the hardware store and buy some paint to cover the dilapidated walls. This new team had unique perspectives and skills that would come together over time to achieve their shared goal. But in the meantime, with no clear first step, they did the only thing they could think of: found a problem and got to work.

Within two years, Hamdi had perfected his recipe and it was just like his mother had made. They launched as Chobani and hired back most of the original 55 employees, then many hundreds more. Just three years later, the company hit $1 billion in annual sales. A decade after Chobani first hit shelves, it accounted for 50% of all yogurt sales in the United States.[20]

There are some elements of the Chobani story that aren't unique. For instance, every company can point to a few lucky breaks or serendipitous alignment of the stars. But what *is* unique is that at the heart of all the success that eventually came was a small team with a unified vision. A shared determination to tackle the pile of problems that had scared everyone else away. A sense of purpose. A belief in something bigger than themselves. Hamdi didn't have much to offer employees in the beginning—no fancy perks, no big incentives, no delusions of grandeur. All he had to offer were some paintbrushes and an opportunity for meaningful work.

And that was enough.

View from a Fishbowl

We're going to go out on a limb and say the best cultures might be formed when there are fewer perks. Google founder Sergey Brin loves to say "scarcity brings clarity." So many great moments in technology come from times where teams had to come together and be resourceful, rather than work from a place of abundance.

My (Justin here, hi!) graduate school experience was like this (I suspect most grad students would agree). The Brown Computer

Science department felt nothing like a modern tech company campus. In my time there, eight of us piled into a single office called the fishbowl. The desks and chairs were terrible. Mine had one arm that could not stay in place, so at least twice a day I'd completely lose my balance and literally fall out of my chair. Our computers were fine but not great; everyone used their own rather than what the department gave us. The carpet couldn't have been cleaned more than once a year, and there were random scraps of "things" everywhere. I remember a pile of loose chargers from the robotics team's modified Roombas appearing on my desk one morning.

None of that mattered though. We were a group of people that would never have come together otherwise. Neehar from India, Justin from Hong Kong, David from New Jersey, Jessie and Greg from Pennsylvania, Laura from Spain, and me from Arkansas. We were all so motivated to get on the forefront of technology and learn together. We all took a few of the same classes, notoriously hard ones, where we had no idea what we were getting into.

The fishbowl became a second home for us.

Hong Kong Justin seemingly never left the office and was laser focused on his PhD, not classes. He would stack empty Starbucks cups on his desk until they reached the ceiling or fell over; it was his measure of productivity. We were all in awe of how focused he was. Grades don't matter in grad school, so he would ask professors what the bare minimum was in order to pass, and then just do that, so he could focus on his dissertation. It worked. Justin won the Association for Constraint Programming's award for outstanding dissertation.

David wore a New York Yankees jacket every day, no matter how cold (or hot) it was. We had a project to recognize each other's faces in a class photo. Something about David's face easily matched everyone else's. I'll always remember the night all of us spent together seeing him pop up for everyone, and our (joyful) consternation when we just couldn't fix it. It was a shared moment of pain that only we'd feel, and solve together. David would do baseball analysis on the side, just like Daryl Morey did for basketball. He kept sending them to the

Yankees. After grad school, he worked as a software engineer for a few years, kept doing baseball analysis, and eventually he joined the Yankees. Now he runs their analysis team.

Laura is a professor now. Greg started a company acquired by Apple. Neehar returned to India and started a health care company. I don't know for sure, but I imagine if you asked any of us, they would call the fishbowl a turning point in our professional lives. You'd be hard-pressed to find a more motivated group of people in an environment entirely free of perks. And it made all the difference. We were all each other had, and we benefited from that scarcity.

This is a story that repeats itself in technology. Diverse groups of people come together, the environment seems about as unlikely as any to breed success, and yet somehow it does.

Ambition + Resourcefulness

At the heart of most successful teams are ambition and resourcefulness. Ambition toward a common goal, and a commitment to getting there, no matter what it takes. The origin story of Silicon Valley is one that most people who flock there now seem not to know.

Robert Noyce was known as the Mayor of Silicon Valley. In the 1950s he moved to California to join Shockley Semiconductor, an upstart founded by pioneering physicist William Shockley, who would go on to win the Nobel Prize for coinventing the semiconductor. The dominant computing model was very different. Massive machines powered by vacuum tubes were state of the art. The modern semiconductor was brand new. The field was moving, and Shockley was at the forefront. Noyce fell in love with the semiconductor, and he saw the future in Shockley's work. Both scientists were enthralled at the opportunity and found their mission.

So Noyce jumped at the chance to join Shockley Semiconductor. It was based in the Santa Clara Valley south of San Francisco, where land was cheap, and it was economically viable for smaller companies to build out the expensive, resource-intensive computing infrastructure of the time.

Increasingly frustrated at how Shockley ran Shockley Semiconductor, a group of eight banded together to strike out on their own. In 1957, this group met one weekend morning in San Francisco to hatch a plan. They would be the first Silicon Valley start-up, before the phrases "Silicon Valley" or "start-up" existed. There was no fancy legal agreement; the team just signed eight one-dollar bills as a contract to each other. And Noyce led the group, which would be called Fairchild Semiconductor.

In this group of eight were Noyce and Gordon Moore, who famously coined the term Moore's Law. After Fairchild, both men would join forces with Andy Grove to start Intel. Among the eight was Eugene Kleiner, who would invest in Intel and then go on to start Kleiner Perkins, one of the first venture capital firms in Silicon Valley.

These people set the tone for a different way of doing things. They started with a mission to change computing, and with very few resources, they looked to each other. They had each other and their ambition, and they were emboldened; World War II had just ended, and America was full of ambition. Our nation had a wild mission, to put a man on the moon. That was the backdrop when they got to work, and so it's understandable that there was no time for frivolous perks. It's this culture of ambition and achievement that set the tone for Silicon Valley.

What makes Silicon Valley special is that it leads with technologists. People who are goal-oriented and motivated by progress. There is no time for hierarchy and mediocrity. The business environment that would emerge would be flat, merit-based, fast-paced, progress-oriented.

Everything about that sort of culture is about people, their abilities, their goals. None of that can be bought. It has to be built. And that would set an enduring legacy for generations of companies to come.

7

A Human-Centric Workforce

We believe that businesses thrive when work is a source of fulfillment for employees, and fulfillment emerges when great teams come together for meaningful work and growth. Fulfillment, meaningful work, and growth are personal benchmarks; they mean different things to different people. As a result, many companies chase their tails trying to be all things to all people. But what if the solution is less, not more? As in, what if companies focused in on the one universal thing that underpins those benchmarks?

Whether you call the recent tectonic shifts in our job market the Great Resignation or the Great Reshuffling, they reflect widespread disenchantment with the role work plays in our lives. That disenchantment is as bad for business as it is for people. If we're going to solve this problem, jobs need to meet the aspirations of people as much as people need to meet the requirements of jobs. So much emphasis is put on the latter that the aspirations of people often get lost in the shuffle.

Aspirations are what get us up in the morning and keep us up at night. They're what drive our attitudes, behaviors, and outputs. Imagine if a candidate's aspirations were taken into account during the hiring process. In addition to assessing a candidate's skills and background, their goals and dreams could also be used to not just evaluate the right fit, but the right growth trajectory. Who can this person become within this role? Does that align with where both the candidate and company want to go? Will both parties benefit from the employer–employee relationship? Is there a shared sense of purpose?

It's a simple reframe that adds a crucial layer of humanity. It prioritizes alignment as a crux of the hiring process, decreasing the odds that companies and candidates discover they're mismatched after the fact. It approaches recruitment in the most individual of ways, seeing candidates as unique human beings with hopes, dreams, competencies, and potential. It looks at them not as a resource or a problem, but as a source and an engine. Because that's exactly what they are.

The Frontliners

When Hubert Joly became Best Buy's CEO in 2012, it was in the wake of a staggering $1.7 billion loss in its fiscal fourth quarter (compared to net income of $651 million one year before) and the departure of its previous CEO amid an investigation of an inappropriate relationship with a female employee. As if things couldn't get worse, Best Buy's stock fell 10% the day Joly took over.[1]

It wasn't just the happenings of 2012 that rocked Best Buy; it had been on a steady decline over the previous decade. In 2002, newly minted CEO Brad Anderson made the smart move to buy the Geek Squad—a start-up with 50 agents who provided tech support to customers in their homes, in stores, by phone, or online—but that was offset by less transformative decisions. For one, the purchase of Napster for $121 million to compete with Apple's dominant iTunes would prove to be a mistake as the rebranded, decriminalized paid music service was soon superseded by Spotify and Pandora. Two, the expansion from 600 stores in the United States and Canada to almost 3,900 in 13 countries just prior to the Great Recession. And three, a less than adequate e-commerce experience compared to competitors, most notably Amazon.[2]

Best Buy president Brian Dunn succeeded Anderson as CEO in 2009 and tried to undo much of what had been done. He closed stores, shut down overseas operations, and dumped Napster. But business simultaneously got worse, and quickly. Stores fell into disrepair, the staff became complacent, sales tanked, the stock price dropped, and to maintain some measure of profitability, the company gave up competing on price. Then came Dunn's resignation following his reported indiscretions.

Which brings us back to Hubert Joly. Born and raised in France, he held two master's degrees and spent 25 years at companies like McKinsey & Company and Vivendi, a media conglomerate where he greenlighted *World of Warcraft,* before becoming president and CEO of travel management company CWT, and later, its holding company Carlson Companies. He had been elected a Global Leader for Tomorrow by the World Economic Forum, and honored as one of the 25 Most Influential Executive of the Business Travel Industry in both 2006 and 2009.[3]

But when he took the reins at Best Buy in 2012, he did so as someone with no retail experience. There were plenty of skeptics that pointed that out, but undeterred, his message to investors and the public alike (well before Donald Trump used something similar on the campaign trail) was "Make Best Buy great again."

Stakeholders encouraged him to use the typical recipe for large-scale turnarounds—cut costs, close stores, fire a bunch of people—but Joly said no, citing that the definition of madness was doing the same thing over and over again and hoping for a different outcome. And that's when he made the most powerful, surprising, and broadly applicable decision: he needed to change the company's approach to managing its people.

In retrospect we can see that Joly was, for lack of a better phrase, a man of the people. When he became CEO, he gave up the executive suite (including secure entrance and panic room) where his predecessor had worked. He reinstated employee discounts, which the same predecessor had eliminated. He worked in stores for a week—complete with blue shirt, khakis, and a badge that read "CEO in Training"—so he could spend time with the staff, whom he called the "frontliners." He saw firsthand the low morale, the disconnection, and the dispiriting Results-Only Work Environment (ROWE) program that revolved around schedules, mandatory meetings, and clock-watching. He heard from store managers about how stressful it was to be expected to measure 40–50 KPIs and from employees about how deflating it felt to speak with a customer for 30 minutes to only have them leave empty-handed (a practice known as "showrooming"). He sensed the indifference when it came to the work everyone did and the company they worked for.

Following these insights, he decided that the overarching question guiding the attempted resurgence of Best Buy—how do we get revenue and margins to go up instead of down?—was the wrong question. He felt that the fate of the company came down to a different question: How do we become more human?

He told the *New York Times,* "If you think about business by first thinking about how you want to be remembered as a human being, most of us gravitate to the golden rule—doing something good to our people."[4] He believed that if Best Buy could connect that desire with the way it ran the business, the employees would love the company and, in turn, so would customers. If Best Buy focused on creating a joyous, growth-oriented culture, they could provide a very human environment where everyone felt that they belonged; a human organization that emphasized individual development.

The plan Joly then put into motion was so simple, so rudimentary, we can only imagine it raised eyebrows among leadership. It started with general managers asking each associate about their personal dreams. Those associates were then encouraged to write their answers on a whiteboard in the break room for everybody to see—a nod to goal accountability, hope, empathy, and interpersonal connection. At a Best Buy store in Boston, one employee wrote that he wanted to buy a house for his family. The manager told him that his job was to help him achieve that dream, and they'd work together to help him develop his skills and move up in the company.

Can you imagine how important, how inspired, and how *seen* that employee must have felt? How motivated he must have been to get back on the floor and be proactive in his work? As if what he did mattered. More importantly, as if *he* himself mattered.

Next was building genuine human connections. One day, Best Buy closed all its stores for a few hours. Store personnel broke into small groups and were given two prompts. The first: share your life story with each other. Joly later recounted listening to a young woman who had been in an abusive relationship with an ex-boyfriend and had been homeless. Best Buy was her home, her family. All of a sudden, he saw her as a human being instead of an employee. The second prompt: share about an inspiring friend. People spoke about their siblings, coworkers, childhood friendships, neighbors. They discussed what it was that made those people inspiring and how it made each of them feel after being around them.

Afterwards, the way forward was obvious and as simple as Joly's plan itself: We're going to treat each other as human beings and treat customers as if we're their inspiring friend.

This manifested in several ways. First, employees were encouraged to do things for each other and for customers that nobody told them to do. For example, at a Best Buy in Florida, a young mother came in with her son who had received a toy dinosaur for Christmas. The child was in tears because the dinosaur was "sick" (the head was not fully connected to the body). Instead of the associates directing the mother and son to the toy aisle to buy a replacement, they brought the injured T. Rex to a service counter and performed "surgery" on the toy, giving the child step-by-step explanations as to what they were doing, as they surreptitiously traded it out for the new one. Was that a standard operating procedure at Best Buy? No! What the associates did came from the heart, and the real triumph was that they felt they had the latitude to do it.

Second, Joly brought back the price-matching guarantee, giving employees the ability to match prices in stores for those found online. This was not only empowering for the employees, but helped prevent shoppers from checking out Best Buy's products in stores before buying it more cheaply on the web. While this was costly to Best Buy, the boost in sales eventually compensated for the cost of matching prices.

Third, a catch-all, courtesy of a new internal mandate: Be human. Customers didn't want salespeople, they wanted someone who could patiently and knowledgably guide them to the best technology products for their needs. Employees who interacted with the customer and got to know them would see them not as a wallet, but as a human being. If price competitiveness was the cost of entry to the game, they would win on advice, convenience, and service.

Joly's people-centric turnaround included far more than what we just covered. He also did away with the ROWE program, offered more benefits like behavioral health coverage and wellness programs, started an intramural sports league, and invested in the engagement and proficiency of the sales associates through one-on-one coaching. In the process, he created a genuine human connection between employee and employer, which organically transferred to the connection between employee and customer.

When Joly stepped down as CEO in 2019, Best Buy had posted five consecutive years of sales growth and its stock price had quadrupled. It had a 25.8% non-GAAP return on investment, up from 10.5% in 2013. It had doubled US online sales from 2012, to $6.5 billion.[5] But to anyone who would listen, Joly insisted that those financial results were achieved by focusing on a purpose bigger than money.

The Proposition

Every company has a customer value proposition; a clear and compelling reason why customers should choose their product or service over that of their competitors. Defining that value has been a popular practice for companies since the 1980s, helping them to establish their target audience, competitive edge, and the specific benefits of their market offering. And then in the early 2000s, companies turned their attention to a new kind of explication: how to market their company to prospective talent and retain them in a competitive job market.

An employee value proposition (EVP) is a common subset of company branding and represents everything of value that the employer has to offer its workers. This internally focused promise defines what employees will get in return for their hard work and commitment, typically revolving around such things as pay, benefits, career development, and work environment. It's a statement of intent packaged as a mutually beneficial covenant, but it can only be a win-win situation if the EVP of an organization matches what someone values. And as history has shown, that's more of a moving target than a standardized consensus.

During the nineteenth and twentieth centuries, workers valued safety, but the generally agreed-upon rules between workers and organizations were marked by hazardous working conditions, strikes, and sometimes violent clashes. For example, in 1911, when 146 workers died in New York's Triangle Shirtwaist Factory fire amid unsafe working conditions—workers, mostly women, were trapped inside the building because the factory owners had locked exits so that workers couldn't take unauthorized breaks, there was only one fire escape but it collapsed during the rescue effort, bulky machines trapped victims, and only a few buckets of water were on hand to douse the flames—it prompted citizen anger and public outcry. And in 1920, when West Virginia miners in the city of Matewan sought union membership, it resulted in a deadly gunfight between private detectives and workers. Ten people were killed, including Matewan's mayor.[6]

After World War II, greater harmony emerged as labor reforms provided basic protections around workplace safety and unemployment benefits. With basic safety and protection as the new baseline, it opened the door for more advantageous promises to be made and the workers knew it. What they wanted now was stability and security. It was the age of pensions, formality (think suits and ties), and paternalism, and the greatest draw for workers was the promise of long-term employment. So that's exactly what companies offered. In exchange for enduring allegiance, employees were given a near-guarantee of job security.

That was a central tenet of employee value through the late 1980s. But then things shifted, more on the company's side of things than the employees'. The corporate mindset became more profit-focused and not as fixated on worker satisfaction or allegiance. Accordingly, "shareholder capitalism" and a concentration on short-term results started its ascent. It morphed into a performance-driven landscape; gone were the promises of job security. Assurances now revolved around sales quota incentives, 401(k) plans, and a flurry of legislative acronyms that provided protection around health benefits: COBRA, HIPAA, CHIP, GINA, MHPAEA, CHIPRA. The value communicated to employees was, essentially, show up and do good work and we'll make sure some of your basic needs are met.

"Workaholism" was prevalent. Employers expected workers to be more devoted to their jobs than their families, to work long hours, to overdeliver on every output. And workers, in the name of reciprocity, rose to the challenge. It became the norm and was simply expected of people. The popular expression—"Choose a job you love, and you will never have to work a day in your life"—was inspiring but utterly foreign.

That is, until there was another shift. The 2000s were the beginning of the great rethinking of the role work played in our lives, giving rise to the importance of wellness, an accommodating work environment, and proper work-life balance. Accordingly, EVPs became all at once more nuanced and more comprehensive. The problem, though, was that there was so much focus on what companies could give to employees, but arguably not enough attention was given to *why*.

EVPs have long been managed by the same three principles: who (employees), what (exceptional employee experience), and how (delivering features that match employee needs). While an EVP provides a concise plug-and-play formula, it also fosters the disconnect that exists between what companies believe employees are after and what those workers actually want.

For example, a recent study from Deloitte found that executives thought additional benefits would be the best retention strategy for baby boomers, yet it didn't rank among the top three for workers in that age group. Similarly, leaders figured company culture would be the top retention factor for millennials while those younger employers didn't rank it in the top three.[7]

It's hard to stay on top of ever-changing priorities, and even harder to successfully juggle the myriad of solutions that align with those priorities. So why not focus on what's underneath them? As Dr. Serena Reep, a communication and management coach, recalled for a piece on *Fast Company*, when a corporate executive asks her what she recommends they do to change the paradigm of an ineffective corporate culture, she says, "Concentrate on the soil."[8] Concentrating on corporate soil doesn't mean providing "more stuff." It doesn't mean pounding away at the specific task of "motivating people." Rather, it means ensuring they feel connected to the worth of the work itself.

Worthy work isn't just reserved for social good organizations or mission-based companies. It's not limited to frontline or social workers. It doesn't have to include organic products or pro bono services. Worth, used interchangeably here with meaning, can be found across every sector, organization, role, and task. It's only dependent on one thing: Whether the people you hire can find their value within whatever your company is trying to achieve.

It's a good reminder that EVPs are a two-way street, a true balance between what the candidate needs from a company and vice versa. When done right, they're a great way to provide implicit and explicit parameters around who, what, how, and why. But they're also a precise and effective filter that discourages mismatched candidates and attracts those who will go on to survive and thrive at a company.

Reap the Benefits

An unfortunate truth: Unhappy employees are bad for business. Monetarily, they cost companies $550 billion each year in lost revenues, settlements, and various other damages.[9] But it's the nonfinancial effects that are just as devastating: workplace conflicts, eroded employee engagement, absenteeism, contagious toxicity, and unhappy customers, just to name five.

But happy, engaged employees? They perform better on nearly every metric—they're three times more creative, 37% better at sales, 19% more accurate when performing tasks, and benefit from a myriad of health and quality-of-life improvements. Not to mention, their engagement results in 21% greater profitability for their company and an 8% rise in the share price of company stock.[10]

Metrics aside, there are endless benefits for both employees and companies when work isn't just a place to log hours but a place to thrive. When it encourages gumption, authenticity, exploration, and personal development, the most fantastic and unexpected things can happen.

When Richard Montañez got a job as a janitor at Frito-Lay, his duties were pretty straightforward. But one day, his manager asked him to collect and weigh all the product that fell on the factory floor. He was shocked to find that it weighed *a lot*. That night, Montañez went home and started writing a proposal (with his wife's help as he only had a fourth-grade education) on how to fix all the waste areas, and it turned out his plan would help save the plant a couple hundred thousand dollars a year. That janitor was asked to join the savings cost improvement team, which he did, and he credits that confidence-boost for what he did next.

After stopping at a street vendor to get some *elote*, a Mexican street corn doused in chili powder, salt, cotija, lime juice, and crema fresca, Montañez had a revelation: The products his employer made—Lay's, Fritos, Ruffles, Cheetos—were all plain. Despite having a growing base of Latino consumers, the company had yet to consider redefining the products' taste profiles. And that's when he wondered, *what if they put chili powder on a Cheeto?*

Working late one night at the production facility, he scooped up some Cheetos that hadn't yet been dusted in cheese. He took them home and covered them in his own concoction of chili powder and other "secret" spices. When he handed them out to family and friends, the snacks were met with universal enthusiasm. Now all Montañez needed was a bigger audience.

Several weeks before this happened, Frito-Lay CEO Roger Enrico recorded a video message and disseminated it to the company's 300,000 employees as a way to boost morale. In it, he encouraged all employees to "act like an owner." Even the janitor? After Montañez got his idea and tested it out, he called Enrico—you know, to speak owner to owner.

Incredibly, the CEO not only took the call, but listened intently as Montañez told him he'd heeded the call to action, studied the company's products, identified a demand in the market, and even crafted his own test snacks in his kitchen. Enrico loved his initiative, and told Montañez he'd be at the plant in two weeks and asked him to prepare a presentation and pitch it to him and other top senior executives.

Two weeks later, the janitor pitched his idea to some of the most highly qualified executives in America. Afterwards, Enrico turned to Montañez and said, "Put that mop away, you're coming with us." And with that, Flamin' Hot Cheetos was born.

There are so many more examples of employee ingenuity and the transformative effects it can have on companies. Amazon Prime, the exclusive membership that gave customers two-day delivery, was an idea put in the digital employee suggestion box by Amazon engineer Charlie Ward. The Sony PlayStation game console was proposed by junior staff member Ken Kutaragi after he created a chip to make his daughter's Nintendo more powerful and provide a better gaming experience. The swipe-to-unlock feature on Apple's iPhone was the result of employee Freddy Anzures noticing how easy it was to lock and unlock the bathroom door of an airplane toilet—you simply had to swipe, nothing else. "Green" initiatives at Xerox, such as the packaging for colored ink created from 100% post-consumer recycled material and altering the rate at which ink was printed onto paper, were ideas from the "Earth Awards" program, a company-wide challenge for employees to think up innovative solutions towards saving company resources while benefiting the environment.[11]

Equally as impressive as the innovations themselves is that the employees felt empowered enough to actually share their ideas and then bring them to life. To us, it says as much about the company as it does about the employee.

A parallel type of empowerment is when people feel like they can take professional risks. One example is companies that offer tuition reimbursement benefits so their workers can pursue their passions and/or advance their careers. Some companies have restrictions around reimbursement percentage, applicable fields of study, and length of time the worker must stay following the completion of their education, but others don't. Employers like Disney, Starbucks, and Walmart offer 100% tuition reimbursement with no strings attached. Intel does the same, and also has its own in-house training organization, Intel University, that offers over 7,000 courses to all employees. Companies like UPS, Intuit, and Home Depot have a cap on yearly reimbursement amounts, but offer the benefits to part-time employees as well.[12]

Underpinning this support is the acknowledgment that growth is imperative, even if it means investing in someone who leaves. That's because it's an investment in people and their potential, not just a veiled way to benefit the company.

As it happens, someone's full potential often can't be reached unless an opportunity presents itself to do so. That can be in the form of company-backed tuition, an empowering environment, an inspiring mentor, the right network, serendipitous circumstances, or a lightbulb moment—the one where someone realizes they are worthy of doing and being more.

That's what happened to Reshma Saujani. After she graduated from college with majors in Political Science and Speech Communication, she went on to Harvard, where she received a Master of Public Policy, and Yale Law School, where she got her Juris Doctor. She worked as an associate for a law firm defending securities fraud cases, an attorney for an asset management firm, then as general counsel at an investment group. But she wasn't happy. The money was good and allowed her to pay off her student loans and help her parents with their mortgage, but she felt more and more beholden to it, more and more scared. She couldn't shake the feeling that she wasn't giving back to the world in any significant way.

She woke up one morning in her early 30s and felt so unfulfilled; she realized she hadn't been making decisions for herself. She'd spent so much time trying to be the perfect immigrant daughter and was living her life based on others' expectations. She knew it was time for a change, time to do something that mattered. So she quit her job. And became the first Indian American woman to run for Congress.

Unfortunately, she lost the race, and in the process, most of her personal savings. But she refused to go backwards, no longer willing to work in a job she hated for the sake of a paycheck. As she pondered next steps, something kept surfacing. She recalled that when she visited computer science classrooms during her congressional campaign, she only saw boys. Instinctively, she knew that was a problem and didn't understand why no one seemed to be talking about it. Saujani had no experience with coding, but she knew tech jobs were the fastest growing, highest paying jobs in the country. Jobs that could lift entire families up into the middle class, yet girls weren't being prepared for them.

No longer swayed by convention or intimidated by risk, Saujani decided to create the nonprofit Girls Who Code. She bought a URL,

filed the appropriate paperwork, gathered a team of industry experts
to help create a curriculum, and signed up 20 girls for its inaugural
Summer Immersion Program in New York. That was in 2012, and
since then, Girls Who Code has reached 500,000 girls in communities across the United States, Canada, India, and the UK. It has three
separate programs that cater to girls aged 8–25 years old, half of whom
come from historically underrepresented groups. It offers a work
prep program that introduces college-aged students to career path-
ways in technology, connects them with potential mentors and spon-
sors in the industry, and develops their networking skills, helping
115,000 alumni so far.[13]

Saujani is certainly not the first or only person to switch careers
in the name of fulfillment. Ina Garten worked in the White House
Office of Management and Budget before opening a specialty-food
store and becoming known as the Barefoot Contessa. Jack Ma was a
lecturer in English and international trade at Hangzhou Dianzi University in China before founding Alibaba, known as China's version
of Amazon. Rina Einy was a professional tennis player who represented Great Britain in the 1988 Olympics before pursuing a corporate career at JP Morgan on Wall Street and Textyle International.
Ray Kroc was a World War I ambulance driver, real estate agent, and
salesman for a paper cup company prior to building the franchising
empire McDonald's.[14]

These examples show the universal truth that people are capable
of so much, and deserve to be put in positions that allow them to soar.
The positions we're talking about are the proper alignment of worker
and role, mission and aspiration, environment and contribution.

Consider the story of Building 20. It was a shoddily constructed
building intended to house a handful of researchers during World War
II plus six months, yet the temporary structure remained for the next
50 years. The longevity was shocking considering how unsoundly it
was built. It was made out of wood even though that broke the fire
code. Its windows never fit and would sometimes fall out in stiff

winds. The place was hot in the summer, cold in the winter, and drafty all the time. Soot blew in from the city and rain poured in through the roof leaks. Down the halls of the building ran exposed pipes and wires. The plywood walls and ceilings meant scientists could easily punch through their boundaries without permission, which they often did. No department owned it—it was multidisciplinary and its tiny offices made it so people would go into the long corridors and share ideas. It became known as an idea factory; an altar for creativity and discovery.

Among the formal achievements of those who worked in Building 20 were the creation of radar, the construction of the world's first atomic clock, and the start of the modern school of linguistics under the impetus of Noam Chomsky. One of the earliest atomic particle accelerators was built there; Amar Bose reinvented the speaker there; and Harold Edgerton, the master of stop-action photography, set up his strobes and cameras in this space to photograph the now-famous bullet shot through an apple.

The building that became a home for almost 4,000 researchers in 20 disciplines and influenced decades of extremely important innovation wasn't actually about the building at all. It was what it represented, what it fostered, what it allowed. By bringing together the right people with the right resources in the right atmosphere, history was made and its significance was evident at its wake. Yes, mourners of the building held a wake. Scientists traveled from around the country to mark the passing and pay their respects to what they called "the plywood palace."

The stories of Montañez, Saujani, and Building 20 are just three examples of what can happen when work is a source of fulfillment. Employees' aspirations are in line with the work itself. They feel inspired and empowered. Productivity and engagement go up. Teams are united. Businesses flourish and industries thrive. It. Is. Possible. But only if the soil beneath the employees infuses them with the belief that it is.

The Woman Named Steve

When Dame Stephanie Shirley was five years old, she boarded a Kindertransport train in Vienna, via a rescue effort that saved nearly 10,000 Jewish children from Nazi Europe. She was taken to England and, along with her nine-year-old sister, placed in the care of foster parents. As Shirley grew up, she knew how lucky she was to have been saved, and as a result, decided to make her life one worth saving.

The 1940s and 1950s were eras historically devoid of opportunity and equality for women. As a kid, Shirley loved mathematics, but the all-girls high school she attended didn't teach it. So she marched right into the headmaster's office and requested permission to take those lessons at the local boys' school, which was granted. When it came time for her to go to university, she opted out since botany was the only science then available to her gender. Instead, she sought employment in a math/technical environment, ultimately landing a job at the Dollis Hill Research Station building computers from scratch and writing code in machine language. Truly impressive for someone who was self-taught and truly unexpected for a woman in a man's world.

Once universities opened more fields of study to female students, she took evening classes for six years to obtain a mathematics degree. She got married, took a job at CDL Ltd, the designer of the ICT 1301 computer, and gave birth to a son. The life of a working mom was hard indeed, and it didn't help that she was experiencing extreme sexism at work. One day, after being fondled and pushed against the wall by a male coworker, she'd had enough. She gave notice, and with only £6 in investment capital, she decided to start a women-only software company, Freelance Programmers.

The odds were stacked against her. For one, software at the time was given away free with hardware. Nobody thought there was a market for software, and certainly not from a woman. And two, staffing a company with only women was a crazy notion. A woman's place was in the home. Women couldn't even open a bank account without their husband's permission, so what made Shirley think she could build a successful company with such inherently *limited* employees?

In the face of such doubt and criticism, she did what any driven, stubborn, and self-respecting entrepreneur would do: She became a pioneer.

Back in those days, social convention expected women to stop working once they got married or once they were expecting. As Shirley saw it, there was a computing world full of people with experience who were being ignored by the workforce. She decided to normalize the concept of women going back to work after a career break. She recruited professionally qualified women who'd left the industry after marriage or childbirth and designed an organizational structure so they could work from home. She disguised the domestic and part-time nature of the staff by offering fixed prices per task instead of hours worked, one of the very first to do so. She established new, flexible work methods like job shares, unfixed hours, and profit-sharing. And just for good measure, she changed her name from "Stephanie" to "Steve" on her business development letters as a way to get through the door before anyone realized that *he* was a *she*.

The team of female programmers she employed wrote code by hand—usually machine code, sometimes binary code—which was sent by mail to a data center to be punched onto paper tape and then re-punched in order to verify it. They worked on operational research, including lots and lots of stock control (ironic since women weren't permitted to work *on* the stock exchange). They developed software standards on management control protocols, eventually adopted by NATO. They programmed the black box flight recorder of the Supersonic Concorde. Who could have imagined all of that could be done by a bunch of women working in their own homes? Dame Stephanie "Steve" Shirley did.

Shirley's success can be attributed to many things. Her early childhood trauma informed her resilience. Her innate intelligence trumped the scarce educational opportunities of the time. Her marginalization as a woman fueled her desire for equality. Her experiences in the male-dominated business world showed her the need for female leadership. But one of the most profound reasons she found success was also one of the most simple: She wanted her team to succeed too.

When she opened one of the earliest software start-ups in Britain to create job opportunities exclusively for women, it was because she *saw* them. She was one of them. She fundamentally understood what they were up against and knew the obstacles in their way. They all wanted the same things—respect, opportunity, and a way to contribute to something greater than what women were allocated by society. With all that collective ambition and shared purpose, Freelance Programmers found steady growth and soon had enough work to staff a dozen women.

In 1975, 13 years after launching the company, equal opportunity legislation in Britain made it illegal to have their pro-female policies. So they welcomed men into the company they'd built. And by "they" we mean all the women owners; Shirley had implemented an employee-owned model and put a quarter of the company into the hands of the staff. When the company went public in 1996, it was valued at $3 billion and 70 of its staff became millionaires.[15]

Growing a company from nothing is one of the hardest and most admired tasks in business. More important than finding financial backing is finding people who believe in the idea and have the right skills and drive to bring it to life. That's precisely what Shirley did, and its importance can't be ignored. Despite no funding, no investors, and no office, she started her empire from her dining room table with the equivalent of what would only be $150 today. Its entire growth strategy centered around the team; their mutual aspirations, their professional competencies, and their dedication to soldier through discrimination.

Dame Stephanie Shirley went on to become one of the most celebrated and respected tech entrepreneurs in Britain's history. She was awarded honorary doctorates from 31 different universities in the UK, including University of Buckingham and University of Cambridge. She established The Shirley Foundation and, as of 2019, made social investments of more than $15 million in IT, including the founding of the Oxford Internet Institute. Another $50 million from her Foundation has gone toward pioneering services for autism, her late son's condition. Among them are Prior's Court, a residential school for autistic students, Autism at Kingwood, which provides support services for adults on the spectrum, and Autistica, which funds research on autism and related conditions.[16]

She and her loyal team shared an unshakable bond; they were committed to each other and to enacting change. They measured success in social—not financial—terms; their eventual windfall was an outcome, not a goal. While the initial team retired long ago and the company went on to be acquired in 2007, their bond will always remain and their collective life motto will always be their guide: "Think for yourself but not of yourself."[17]

Who Is How

The way that people think about work is changing. A lack of fulfillment in people's current jobs has led to the Great Resignation and a very real shift in how people think about the future of work. With this workforce evolution, people are seeking purpose-led employment to feel more fulfilled. That presents an exciting opportunity for companies to reimagine their hiring process as one that ensures a fulfilling match for both employees and companies.

As we said before, jobs need to meet the aspirations of people as much as people need to meet the requirements of jobs. Recruiters tap into this dynamic at the first point of contact—the hire. From outreach to offer, recruiters and hiring managers have outsized power to make a meaningful difference in whether or not people find work that matches their skills and goals. That's why we believe that recruitment is a vital part of fulfillment in the workplace and, more broadly, the future of work.

Finding talent has never been easy, and it's harder than ever today. Talented people aren't breaking through to the work they most want to do, and companies aren't finding the candidates who best align with their missions. The current hiring market is competitive, expensive, and doesn't result in either party—employers or employees—reaching their full potential. Yet everyone's still relying on the same, outdated recruitment processes that only perpetuates the widespread dissatisfaction.

In a business world that focuses so much on the *how*—five-year plans, strategies, projections, marketing, product differentiation—far too few focus on the true foundation of a successful operation: the people. *Who* you have on your team is the most imperative yet under-appreciated determinant of growth and success. The only *how* that's applicable here is how you're going to find them.

Acknowledgments

From Justin Palmer:

This book is all about team. So my biggest thanks go to everyone who's helped build Teamable over the past five years. It's been nothing short of a life-changing experience to build a company from scratch with a group of such talented, motivated, delightful people.

We've experienced incredible highs and lows together. Going through that has made us all better, and knowing you, working with you, is a huge part of who I am. I love that we got the opportunity to write this book. Jessica and I are listed as authors of this book, but this is about our team, and a moment where we can share some of the things that we learned.

Dima Lashkov, Bruce Minner, Jared Sohn, Jessica Schertz, Jeff Von Ward, Zac Horn, Doreen Ghafari, you were there in the earliest days building Teamable. Thanks for the opportunity to work together. You're the heart of what we have built. What we have done together is a huge feat. I'm incredibly proud to have done it alongside you. Our team keeps me going and inspires me every day.

We get to build something that has transformed so many companies, and so many people's working lives. People join teams they are really excited about and make their life's work a reality, in small part, thanks to help from what we have put together. The fact that we also got to experience the same thing, while helping others do the same, is amazing. I love the impact of what we have done, and I love that we did this together.

Our ideas needed some help coming to life. To Krista Morgan, thank you. Your insight, hard work, patience, and vision made this book work. You took the time to learn about us, our space, and what we do. Your thinking pushed us forward in the best possible ways. We would not have made this book happen without you. To Evan Leatherwood and your team, you pushed us to think bigger about what we do and elevate our story. Thank you.

I'm grateful to so many mentors. Eduardo Vivas, Dan Portillo, Ross Fubini, you guys stand out. Thanks for being great investors, especially with your time, knowledge, and friendship. You've been so generous, helpful, wise, patient, and kind over the years. Thank you.

Thanks to my incredibly supportive wife, Anne, and pup, Penny. You've always been my biggest fans, behind me and my dreams, and you've experienced the highs and lows of my journey right alongside me. I love you.

From Jessica Schertz:

We set out to tell a story about data and technology. How people we don't know can build teams of people we'll never meet. And while we did accomplish that, it became so clear with each chapter that we'd learned just as much from our own story than we ever could from what millions of data points can tell us.

It's rare in Silicon Valley to spend years building something with the same team. It's even rarer to build alongside people who are guided by teamwork and curiosity, and never ego. What an incredible adventure it's been, working with such inspiring people to create something so incredible from scratch. It's impossible to imagine any of this (the product, the team, or the culture) without the early (and continued) impact from Jared, Bruce, Joe, Ray, Mike, Dima, or Jeff.

It's an unusual story, for which no one deserves more credit than Justin. Thank you for creating an environment that's always encouraged us to chase a crazy idea, give it our best shot, dust ourselves off and try again if it didn't work out like we'd hoped. The unwavering faith you have in the team gives us the freedom to find new solutions to hard problems.

So many thanks to Krista, for helping us tell our story and talking data with me (or is it pronounced "data"?). Also to Dominika, Kevin, Dan, and so many others who make the work fun. Everyone should be lucky enough to build something with a team so determined to help each other succeed.

And to my family—Chris, Sam, and Cal. You were my first "job" that lit my soul on fire and taught me to never sacrifice my time on anything I wasn't totally enamored with. The days have been long, but the years have been so short. The balancing act of raising a family while growing a company was never easy, but always worth it.

Notes

Chapter One: A Matter of Intention

1. Perez, S., 2020, "Quibi gains 300K launch day downloads, hits No. 3 on App Store," TechCrunch, April 7, https://techcrunch. com/2020/04/07/quibi-gains-300k-launch-day-downloads-hits-no-3-on-app-store/
BBC News, 2020, "Quibi reaches 1.7m downloads in the first week," April 13, https://www.bbc.com/news/technology-52275692
2. Blankfeld, K., 2016, "Katzenberg net worth climbs to nearly $900 million after Comcast buys Dreamworks Animation," *Forbes*, August 26, https://www.forbes.com/sites/kerenblankfeld/2016/ 08/26/katzenberg-net-worth-climbs-to-nearly-900-million-after-comcast-buys-dreamworks-animation/?sh=41ad70af7b66
Alexander, J., 2020, "Quibi has raised close to $2 billion, and it hasn't even launched yet," The Verge, May 4, https://www.theverge .com/2020/3/4/21165312/quibi-funding-investors-jeffrey-katzenberg-launch-date-price
3. Schmidt, A., 2020, "How Meg Whitman turned eBay into a multi-billion dollar company," *Fox Business*, May 10, https://www.fox business.com/money/meg-whitman-ebay-defining-moment
4. Novet, J., 2019, "HPE's stock falls as revenue comes up short," CNBC, November 25, https://www.cnbc.com/2019/11/25/ hewlett-packard-enterprise-hpe-earnings-q4-2019.html

5. Katzenberg, J. and Whitman, M., 2020, "Quibi open letter," *Medium*, October 21, https://quibi-hq.medium.com/an-open-letter-from-quibi-8af6b415377f

6. Singh, R., 2008, "History of recruiting: Part I," ERE, January 25, https://www.ere.net/history-of-recruiting-part-i/
Dochev, M., n.d., "Ancient recruitment," *Found* (blog), retrieved July 5, 2022, from https://www.found-rg.com/blog/2020/12/ancient-recruitment

7. Zane, M., 2022, "What is the working age population in the US?" [2022]: "Statistics on prime working age population in America," Zippia, March 1, https://www.zippia.com/advice/working-age-population/

8. MRINetwork, 2017, "2017 recruiter sentiment study," https://mrinetwork.com/media/304094/2017hiringsentimentstudy.pdf

9. US Census Bureau, 2020, "US Census Bureau releases new educational attainment data," https://www.census.gov/newsroom/press-releases/2020/educational-attainment.html

10. Schultz, Sydney Ellen and Schultz, Duane, 2010, *Psychology and Work Today*, New York: Prentice Hall: 61.

11. Beard, A., 2019, "Experience doesn't predict a new hire's success," *Harvard Business Review*, Sept./Oct., https://hbr.org/2019/09/experience-doesnt-predict-a-new-hires-success

12. McKinsey & Company, 2020, "Diversity Wins: How Inclusion Matters," https://www.mckinsey.com/~/media/mckinsey/featured%20insights/diversity%20and%20inclusion/diversity%20wins%20how%20inclusion%20matters/diversity-wins-how-inclusion-matters-vf.pdf

13. US Bureau of Labor Statistics, "Employment—Population Ratio—Women," retrieved October 17, 2022, from FRED Federal Reserve Bank of St. Louis, https://fred.stlouisfed.org/series/LNS12300002

14. GetLatka, n.d., "How Figma hit $190M revenue with 50K customers in 2022," retrieved July 3, 2022, from https://getlatka.com/companies/figma

15. WorkOS, 2021, "How Zendesk used enterprise features to grow from $1 million to $1 billion in 12 years," *WorkOS* (blog), https://workos.com/blog/zendesk-enterprise-features

16. Mirzadegan, J., (host), 2021, "CCO Figma, Amanda Kleha: The Strategies Behind Figma's $10 Billion Valuation," podcast episode, August 2, *Grit*, https://open.spotify.com/episode/13nPEUQpvxkMheNYbpyL3r

17. Simonds, L., 2022, "Figma's Dylan Field will discuss evolving as a leader and why fun is an essential company value at TechCrunch Disrupt," TechCrunch, June 8, https://techcrunch.com/2022/06/08/figmas-dylan-field-will-discuss-evolving-as-a-leader-and-why-fun-is-an-essential-company-value-at-techcrunch-disrupt

Mathews, J., 2022, "After Adobe agrees to a $20B acquisition, Figma's earliest investors detail the path to exit," *Fortune*, September 16, https://fortune.com/2022/09/16/adobe-figma-acquisition-earliest-investors-path-exit/

18. Fernández-Aráoz, C., 2014, June, "21st-century talent spotting," *Harvard Business Review*, https://hbr.org/2014/06/21st-century-talent-spotting

19. Fernández-Aráoz, "21st-century talent spotting."

20. Ladders, 2018, "Eye-tracking study," https://www.theladders.com/static/images/basicSite/pdfs/TheLadders-EyeTracking-StudyC2.pdf

"Katzenberg and Whitman brought to the table a laundry list": Hansell, S., 2002, "Meg Whitman and eBay, net survivors," *New York Times*, May 5.

Holson, L., 1999, "Defining the on-line chief; Ebay's Meg Whitman explores management, web style," *New York Times*, May 10.

"Industry proficiency aside, Katzenberg and Whitman's shared understanding": Collis, D. J. and Shu, T., 2021, "(180) Days of Quibi," HBS No. 722-377, Harvard Business School Publishing, October, http://hbr.org/product/-180--Days-of-Quibi/an/722377-PDF-ENG

"Two decades ago, companies began adding degree requirements": Fuller, J. B., Langer, C., Nitschke, J., O'Kane, L., Sigelman, M., and Taska, B., 2022, "The emerging degree reset," The Burning Glass Institute, retrieved July 7, 2022, from https://www.hbs.edu/managing-the-future-of-work/Documents/research/emerging_degree_reset_020922.pdf

"Today, a growing number of companies, including many in tech": Association of American Colleges and Universities, 2018, Survey: "Fulfilling the American Dream: Liberal education and the future of work," https://www.aacu.org/research/fulfilling-the-american-dream-liberal-education-and-the-future-of-work

"It was replaced in 1997 by an online equivalent": Mariani, M., 1999, "Replace with a database: O★NET replaces the Dictionary of Occupational Titles," *Occupational Outlook Quarterly*, Spring, https://www.bls.gov/careeroutlook/1999/Spring/art01.pdf

Chapter Two: Diverse Intangibles

1. Favale, D., 2011, "10 most underrated players in the NBA," *Bleacher Report*, November 10, https://bleacherreport.com/articles/933315-10-most-underrated-players-in-the-nba

2. NBA Advanced Stats, n.d., "All time leaders," retrieved July 15, 2022 from https://www.nba.com/stats/alltime-leaders

3. TED, 2018, "The best teams have this secret weapon," video, YouTube, May 31, https://www.youtube.com/watch?v=hPgY45xsGsU

4. Ansberry, C., 2019, "Reach for the moon: Four lives, the space race and a chaotic decade," *Wall Street Journal*, July 14, https://www.wsj.com/articles/how-the-moon-landing-shaped-four-americans-lives-11563152941

5. Atkinson, N., 2010, "13 things that saved Apollo 13, Part 10: Duct tape," Universe Today, April 26, https://www.universetoday.com/63673/13-things-that-saved-apollo-13-part-10-duct-tape/

6. Kranz, G., 2009, *Failure Is Not an Option: Mission Control from Mercury to Apollo 13 and Beyond*, Simon and Schuster: 393.

7. Keller, Scott and Meaney, Mary, 2017, *Leading Organization: Ten Timeless Truths*, New York: Bloomsbury.

8. Hempel, J., 2015, "Restart," *Wired*, January, https://www.wired .com/2015/01/microsoft-nadella/
   Chmielewski, D., 2018, "Hulu unveils sweeping reorganization: Chief content officer Joel Stillerman, two more execs out," *Deadline*, June 1, https://deadline.com/2018/06/hullu-reorganization -new-chief-technical-officer-appoints-chief-data-officer-in-reor ganization-1202401925/
   O'Kane, S., 2018, "Tesla lays off thousands of workers as part of a 'company-wide restructuring,'" *The Verge*, June 12, https://www .theverge.com/2018/6/12/17454004/elon-musk-tesla-layoffs- restructuring

9. Mariotti, A., Robinson, S., and Esen, E., 2017, "2017 Human Capital Benchmarking Report," Society for Human Resources Man- agement, https://www.shrm.org/hr-today/trends-and-forecasting/ research-and-surveys/Documents/2017-Human-Capital- Benchmarking.pdf
   Mahan, T. F., Nelms, D. A., Jeeun, Y., Jackson, A., Hein, M., and Moffett, R., 2020, "2020 retention report: Insights on 2019 turn- over trends, reasons, costs & recommendations," Work Institute, https://workinstitute.com/retention-report/

10. Rivera, L., 2015, "A tilted playing field," KelloggInsight, https:// insight.kellogg.northwestern.edu/article/a-tilted-playing-field

11. Hunt, D.V., Layton, D., and Prince, S., 2015, "Why diversity mat- ters," McKinsey & Company, https://www.mckinsey.com/~/ media/mckinsey/business%20functions/people%20and%20org- anizational%20performance/our%20insights/why%20diversity%20 matters/diversity%20matters.pdf

12. Lee, C. S., Therriault, D. J., and Linderholm, T., 2012, "On the cognitive benefits of cultural experience: Exploring the relation- ship between studying abroad and creative thinking," *Applied Cognitive Psychology* 26: 768–778, https://doi.org/10.1002/ acp.2857

Benet-Martínez, V., Lee, F., and Leu, J., 2006, "Biculturalism and cognitive complexity expertise in cultural representations," *Journal of Cross-Cultural Psychology* 37: 386–407, https://doi.org/10.1177/0022022106288476

Hong, L., and Page, S. E., 2004, "Groups of diverse problem solvers can outperform groups of high-ability problem solvers," *Proceedings of the National Academy of Sciences* 101, no. 46: 16385–16389, https://doi.org/10.1073/pnas.0403723101

13. Sommers, S. R., 2006, "On racial diversity and group decision-making: Identifying multiple effects of racial composition on jury deliberations," *Journal of Personality and Social Psychology* 90, no. 4: 597–612, https://doi.org/10.1037/0022-3514.90.4.597

14. Ignatius, A., 2021, "I'm here because I'm as good as you," *Harvard Business Review*, July-August, https://hbr.org/2021/07/im-here-because-im-as-good-as-you

15. Xerox, n.d., "Xerox history timeline," retrieved August 1, 2022, from https://www.xerox.com/en-us/about/history-timeline

16. SocialTalent, n.d., "9 companies around the world that are embracing diversity in a BIG way," *SocialTalent* (blog), retrieved August 1, 2022, from https://www.socialtalent.com/blog/diversity-and-inclusion/9-companies-around-the-world-that-are-embracing-diversity

17. Heaslip, M., 2022, "39 awesome companies leading the way in diversity," *Vervoe*, https://vervoe.com/most-diverse-companies/

18. Sanborn, A., 2021, "5 companies that are LGBTQ+ friendly," Work It Daily, https://www.workitdaily.com/lgbtq-friendly-companies/adobe

19. SAP, n.d., "Global diversity and inclusion," retrieved August 1, 2022, from https://www.sap.com/sweden/about/company/our-values/diversity.html

Swaab, R. I., Schaerer, M., Anicich, E. M., Ronay, R., and Galinsky, A. D., 2014, "The too-much-talent effect: Team interdependence determines when more talent is too much or not enough," *Psychological Science* 25, no. 8: 1581–1591, https://doi.org/10.1177/0956797614537280

**"Morey's career did not start in sports management";
"Morey's technology background was perfect for sports":**
NBA, 2006, "Rockets hire Morey as assistant GM," press release,
https://www.nba.com/amp/rockets/news/Rockets_Hire_
Morey_as_Assistan-174585-822.html
"Morey was the NBA's Executive of the Year in 2018":
Newport, K., 2018, "Daryl Morey wins 2018 NBA Basketball
Executive of the Year award," *Bleacher Report*, June 25, https://
bleacherreport.com/articles/2782928-daryl-morey-wins-
2018-nba-basketball-executive-of-the-year-award
**"In reviewing the data, Morey noticed Battier wasn't
grabbing"; "Upon being traded to the Rockets"; "Kobe
Bryant seemingly had no weaknesses to his game":** Lewis,
M., 2009, "The no-stats all-star*," New York Times Magazine*, February 13, https://www.nytimes.com/2009/02/15/magazine/
15Battier-t.html
**"As the Apollo 13 shuttle approached the moon"; "It was
an exercise they could never have accounted for":** Atkinson, N., 2010, "13 things that saved apollo 13, part 10: Duct tape,"
Universe Today, April 26, https://www.universetoday.
com/63673/13-things-that-saved-apollo-13-part-10-duct-tape/
**"These heroes in Mission Control didn't have experience
in space":** Smithsonian National Air and Space Museum. n.d.,
"Apollo 13," retrieved on October 1, 2022, from, https://airandspace.
si.edu/explore/stories/apollo-missions/apollo-13
**"Northwestern Mutual Life, a financial services mutual
organization":** Cascade Team, 2022, "Top 4 cross functional
team examples," *Cascade* (blog), April 14, https://www.cascade
.app/blog/cross-functional-teams-drive-innovation
"CarMax, the largest seller of used cars in the US": Kane,
G. C. and Phillips, A. N. 2017, "Cultivating a culture of cross-
functional teaming and learning at CarMax, *MIT Sloan Management Review*, August 11, https://sloanreview.mit.edu/article/
cultivating-a-culture-of-cross-functional-teaming-and-learning-
at-carmax/

"One of our clients, Scoop Technologies": Karbo.com, n.d., "In The Know | Jonathan Sadow, CGO, Scoop Technologies," interview with karbo.com, retrieved on August 1, 2022, from https://karbocom.com/in-the-know-jonathan-sadow-scoop-technologies-chief-growth-officer/

"Leidos, an American engineering company, focuses on 'neurodiversity'": Brennan, B. and Good, M., 2017, "The cyber workforce, part 2: How we build capacity," Leidos, July 25, https://www.leidos.com/insights/cyber-workforce-part-2-how-we-build-capacity

"Leidos sees the potential of people with these disorders": Piscano, G. P., 2017, "Neurodiversity as a competitive advantage," *Harvard Business Review*, May/June, https://hbr.org/2017/05/neurodiversity-as-a-competitive-advantage

"Abbott, the medical device company headquartered in Chicago": Heaslip, E., 2022, "39 awesome companies leading the way in diversity," Vervoe, August 1, https://vervoe.com/most-diverse-companies/

"Its career page includes a 'military skills translator'": Abbott, n.d. "Veterans at Abbott," retrieved August 1, 2022, from https://www.abbott.com/careers/diversity-and-inclusion/veterans.html

Chapter Three: State of the Union

1. Froelich Tractor Museum, n.d., "The Tractor," retrieved on September 3, 2022, from https://www.froelichtractor.com/the-tractor.html

Biggleswade History Society, n.d., "Dan Albone: The man, family, cyclist, and inventor," retrieved on September 3, 2022, from https://web.archive.org/web/20120315090452/http://www.biggleswadehistory.org.uk/Dan%20Albone.htm

Jones, P. M., 2015, "The science of agriculture," chapter 7 in *Agricultural Enlightenment: Knowledge, Technology, and Nature, 1750–1840*:

161–187, https://doi.org/10.1093/acprof:oso/9780198716075.003 .0008

Harford, T., 2017, January 2, "How fertilizer helped feed the world," BBC, https://www.bbc.com/news/business-38305504

2. Corday, R., 2014, April 24, "The evolution of assemble lines: A brief history," Robohub, https://robohub.org/the-evolution-of-assembly-lines-a-brief-history/

Encyclopedia of Detroit, n.d., "Model T," https://detroithistorical. org/learn/encyclopedia-of-detroit/model-t

3. Tozzi, C., 2021, "Mainframe history: How mainframe computers have changed over the years," *Precisely* (blog), March 5, https:// www.precisely.com/blog/mainframe/mainframe-history

4. Hoffman, P., 2007, *King's Gambit: A Son, A Father, and the World's Most Dangerous Game*, Hyperion.

The Chess Journal, n.d., "How many chess players are there in the world?" Retrieved on September 6, 2022, from https://www. chessjournal.com/how-many-chess-players-are-there/

5. The Chess Journal, "How many chess players are there in the world?" Chess.com, 2020, October 15, "How many hours of chess study does it take to be a grandmaster?" https://www.chess.com/article/ view/chess-grandmaster-hours

6. Li, E., Ouellette, D. J., and Duong, T. Q., 2018, "Differences in subcortical brain volumes between expert and novice chess players," The International Society for Magnetic Resonance in Medicine, https://cds.ismrm.org/protected/18MProceedings/ PDFfiles/2090.html

7. Coffee.org, n.d., "History of Starbucks," retrieved on August 20, 2022, from https://coffee.org/pages/history-of-starbucks

MacArthur, A., 2020, "The real history of Twitter, in brief," Lifewire, November 25, https://www.lifewire.com/history-of-twitter-3288854

Jones, T., 2013, "The surprisingly long history of Nintendo," Gizmodo, September 20, https://gizmodo.com/the-surprisingly-long-history-of-nintendo-1354286257

Gebel, M., 2019, "9 of the biggest pivots in tech history, from Nintendo to Instagram," *Insider*, August 29, https://www.businessinsider.com/tech-company-biggest-pivots-nintendo-instagram-amazon-2019-8

Koebler, J., 2015, "10 years ago today, YouTube launched as a dating website," Vice, April 23, https://www.vice.com/en/article/78xqjx/10-years-ago-today-youtube-launched-as-a-dating-website

Surowiecki, J., 2013, "Where Nokia went wrong," *New Yorker*, September 3, https://www.newyorker.com/business/currency/where-nokia-went-wrong

Kovach, S., 2013, "How Samsung went from a dried fish exporter to one of the top names in tech," *Business Insider*, February 9, https://www.businessinsider.com/history-of-samsung-2013-2

Nazar, J., 2013, "14 famous business pivots," *Forbes*, October 8, https://www.forbes.com/sites/jasonnazar/2013/10/08/14-famous-business-pivots/?sh=7158774a5797

8. Huet, E., 2021, "The pandemic pivot: How three startups transformed during Covid," *Bloomberg*, August 4, https://www.bloomberg.com/news/articles/2021-08-04/pandemic-pivot-how-table22-curative-welcome-transformed-during-covid

9. Tsai, K., 2021, "Mattel sales soared 47% as parents bought toys with stimulus checks, toymaker raises outlook," CNBC, April 22, https://www.cnbc.com/2021/04/22/mattel-mat-q1-2021-earnings.html

10. Red Roof, 2020, "Red Roof offers 'Work Under Our Roof' day rate to provide a comfortable and quiet space for remote workers," press release, March 30, https://www.prnewswire.com/news-releases/red-roof-offers-work-under-our-roof-day-rate-to-provide-a-comfortable-and-quiet-space-for-remote-workers-301031912.html

11. Bicknell, J., 2009, "Reflections on 'John Henry': Ethical issues in singing performance," *The Journal of Aesthetics and Art Criticism*

67, no. 2: 173-180. https://doi.org/10.1111/j.1540-6245.2009. 01346.x

12. World Economic Forum, 2020, October 20, "The Future of Jobs Report 2020," https://www.weforum.org/reports/the-future-of-jobs-report-2020/digest

13. Kasparov, G., 2020, February 21, "As the first knowledge worker whose job was threatened by a machine, I'm happy to share my positive message about the future of the human-machine relationship," @Kasparov63 tweet, Twitter, https://twitter.com/kasparov63/status/1230966327088685058

14. Kilday, B., 2018, "The little known story of how Google Earth helped save more than 400 lives after Hurricane Katrina," LinkedIn, June 1, https://www.linkedin.com/pulse/little-known-story-how-google-earth-saved-more-than-400-kilday/

15. Ford, 2019, September 26, "Ford choreographs robots to help people—and each other—on the Fiesta assembly line," https://media.ford.com/content/fordmedia/feu/en/news/2019/09/26/ford-choreographs-robots-to-help-people--and-each-other--on-the-.html
Greenfield, D., n.d., "BMW outfits robots with artificial intelligence," *Automation World*, retrieved on August 21, 2022, from https://www.automationworld.com/factory/robotics/article/21138274/bmw-outfits-robots-with-artificial-intelligence
Cobot Intelligence, n.d., "Which companies are using collaborative robots to improve production cycles?" Retrieved on August 21, 2022, from https://cobotintel.com/techman-ca/companies-using-collaborative-robots-to-improve-production-cycles/
"With technology and automation progressively affecting jobs": Davis. K., 2020, "Cradle of Cantonese cuisine welcomes robot chef overlords," Sixth Tone, June 24, https://www.sixthtone.com/news/1005845/cradle-of-cantonese-cuisine-welcomes-robot-chef-overlords
"The robotic restaurant was a concept designed"; **"Despite initial intrigue form Heweilai's customers";**

"Behind the scenes, Heweilai leadership": NDTV, 2016, April 7, "Restaurants in China sack 'dumb' robot chefs and waiters," https://www.ndtv.com/world-news/restaurants-in-china-sack-dumb-robot-chefs-and-waiters-1339897

"Japan's Henn na Hotel . . . opened in 2015 with a staff of 250 robots": Diskin, E., 2019, "A Japanese hotel known for its robot staff had to fire half of its droid workforce because they couldn't perform tasks as well as humans," *Insider*, January 25, https://www.insider.com/japanese-hotel-fires-half-of-robot-staff-2019-1

Henn na Hotel, n.d., Hen na Hotel website, retrieved on August 10, 2022, from https://www.h-n-h.jp/en/

"But just three years after it opened, the hotel fired half of its robot "employees": Gale, A. and Mochizuki, T., 2019, "Robot hotel loses love for robots," *Wall Street Journal*, January 14, https://www.wsj.com/articles/robot-hotel-loses-love-for-robots-11547484628

"In recent decades technology has closed the gap even more": Davenport, T. H. and Kirby, J., 2016, *Only Humans Need Apply: Winners and Losers in the Age of Smart Machines*, HarperBusiness.

"A Russian chess grandmaster and former World Chess Champion": Kasparov, G., 2017, *Deep Thinking: Where Machine Intelligence Ends and Human Creativity Begins*, PublicAffairs.

Rasskin-Gutman, D., 2009, *Chess Metaphors: Artificial Intelligence and the Human Mind*, trans. D. Klosky, MIT Press.

"Deep Blue was a chess-playing expert system run on a unique purpose-built IBM supercomputer": IBM, n.d., "Deep Blue," retrieved on September 10, 2022, from https://www.ibm.com/ibm/history/ibm100/us/en/icons/deepblue/

"Deep Blue's win was seen as symbolically significant, a sign that artificial intelligence was catching up to human intelligence": Thompson, C., 2014, "Computers will be like humans by 2029: Google's Ray Kurzweil," CNBC, June 11, https://www.cnbc.com/2014/06/11/computers-will-be-like-humans-by-2029-googles-ray-kurzweil.html

"That observation prompted Austrian economist Joseph Schumpeter to coin the term 'creative destruction'": Hoppock, D. J., 2019, "Insights on creative destruction and technology," Investopedia, June 25, https://www.investopedia.com/articles/investing/070715/insights-creative-destruction-and-technology.asp

"There's an African American folk hero named John Henry": National Park Service, 2020, "The legend of John Henry: Talcott, WV," NPS, New River Gorge, January 22, https://www.nps.gov/neri/planyourvisit/the-legend-of-john-henry-talcott-wv.htm

"Kasparov ultimately saw artificial intelligence as an opportunity for collaboration": Kasparov, G., 2017, "Don't fear intelligent machines. Work with them," video, Ted Conferences, https://www.ted.com/talks/garry_kasparov_don_t_fear_intelligent_machines_work_with_them

"In 2005, an online chess playing site hosted what it called a 'freestyle' chess tournament": Marr, B., 2016, "How soon will you lose your job to an ai robot? . . . or is that the wrong question?" *Forbes*, October 24, https://www.forbes.com/sites/bernardmarr/2016/10/24/how-soon-will-you-lose-your-job-to-an-ai-robot-or-is-that-the-wrong-question/?sh=393a3f283194

"For example, a German factory that produces Adidas running shoes uses robotic technology": Reuters, 2015, December 9, "German robots to manufacture first running shoes for Adidas," https://www.entrepreneur.com/article/253770 Burgess, M., 2020, "Robots are stringing together these Adidas running shoes," *Wired*, October 9, https://www.wired.com/story/robots-are-stringing-together-these-adidas-running-shoes/

"Invented in the mid-90s by professors at Northwestern University, cobots took off": Garcia, J., 2020, "Pandemic fuels global demand for 'cobots' in health sector," Tech Sabado, https://techsabado.com/2020/09/02/pandemic-fuels-global-demand-for-cobots-in-health-sector/

Chapter Four: On the Shoulders of Giants

1. Levy, S., 2011, *In the Plex: How Google Thinks, Works, and Shapes Our Lives*, Simon & Schuster: 30.
2. Oberlo, 2022, "Search engine market share in 2022," https://www.oberlo.com/statistics/search-engine-market-share#
3. Newell Brone, J. and Swain, A., 2012, *The Professional Recruiter's Handbook: Delivering Excellence in Recruitment Practice*, Kogan.
4. Usher, S., 2014, *Letters of Note: An Eclectic Collection of Correspondence Deserving of a Wider Audience*, Chronicle.
5. McNamara, P., 1999, "Monster.com's Super Bowl ads pay off in a big way," CNN.com, http://www.cnn.com/TECH/computing/9902/08/monsterad.idg/index.html
   BeBusinessed, n.d., "History of the online job search," retrieved October 5, 2022, from https://bebusinessed.com/history/history-online-job-search/
6. Frew McMillan, A., 2000, "How to use wires to hook you up and blast your career into the stratosphere," CNNMoney, July 11, https://money.cnn.com/2000/07/11/career/q_webjob/
7. Davis, S. J ., Macaluso, C., and Waddell, S. R., 2021, September, "Economic brief: How do employers recruit new workers?" Federal Reserve Bank of Richmond, https://www.richmondfed.org/publications/research/economic_brief/2021/eb_21-28
   CareerBuilder, 2016, "Back to basics: How to rethink the candidate experience and make better hires," https://hiring-assets.careerbuilder.com/media/attachments/original-2184.pdf
8. Reuters, 2021, October 18, "Facebook plans to hire 10,000 in EU to build 'metaverse,'" https://www.reuters.com/technology/facebook-plans-hire-10000-eu-build-metaverse-2021-10-17/#

Escober, S., 2022, "Amazon to hire 150,000 holiday workers, in line with last year," *Barron's*, October 6, https://www.barrons.com/articles/amazon-jobs-seasonal-hiring-51665059984

Hines, M., 2022, "9 fast-growing Chicago tech companies hiring now," Built In Chicago, March 14, https://www.builtinchicago.org/2022/03/14/9-chicago-companies-hiring-march-2022

Oracle, 2022, June 24, "Oracle cuts the time from job requisition to employment offer by nine days," https://www.oracle.com/customers/oracle-journeys-or-connections/

Bishop, T., 2021, "Microsoft adds 23k employees in one year, growing 14% despite pandemic and tight labor market," GeekWire, October 27, https://www.geekwire.com/2021/microsoft-adds-23k-employees-one-year-growing-14-despite-pandemic-tight-labor-market/

9. Anders, G., 2021, "Can you wait 49 days? Why getting hired takes so long in engineering," LinkedIn, August 4, https://www.linkedin.com/pulse/can-you-wait-49-days-why-getting-hired-takes-so-long-george-anders/

The Brixton Group, n.d., "The state of hiring: How long is it taking to hire in the current job market?" Retrieved on October 6, 2022, from https://www.brixton.net/the-state-of-hiring-how-long-is-it-taking-to-hire-in-the-current-job-market?

De Lara, K., Holden, L., and Trigg, M., 2018, "2018 recruiting trends report," Entelo, https://cdn2.hubspot.net/hubfs/202646/Entelo's%202018%20Recruiting%20Trends%20Report.pdf

Reiners, B., 2022, "How to sell candidates while assessing their fit," Built In, May 31, https://builtin.com/tech-recruiter-resources/how-to-sell-candidates-while-assessing-their-fit

10. Bureau of Labor Statistics, 2022, May 9, "The economics daily: Number of unemployed people per job opening is 0.5 in March 2022," https://www.bls.gov/opub/ted/2022/number-of-unemployed-people-per-job-opening-is-0-5-in-march-2022.htm

Bureau of Labor Statistics, 2022, "Employment projections—2021–2031," press release, September 8, https://www.bls.gov/news.release/pdf/ecopro.pdf

ManpowerGroup, n.d., "The talent shortage," retrieved on October 7, 2022, from https://go.manpowergroup.com/talent-shortage

"The first officially documented recruitment agency was started by Henry Robinson": McKeon, M., 2006, *The Secret History of Domesticity: Public, Private, and the Division of Knowledge*, John Hopkins University Press.

"Dumont led the way in selling TV sets when they were new devices": Chase, B., 2020, *Strategy First: How Businesses Win Big*, Greenleaf.

"For one, Google ranked search results using a trademarked algorithm called PageRank": Varagouli, E., 2020, December 23, "Everything you need to know about Google PageRank (why it still matters)," *Semrush* (blog), https://www.semrush.com/blog/pagerank/

"Candidates were encouraged to write resumes": Collins, D., 2011, "The 500-year evolution of the resume," *Business Insider*, February 12, https://www.businessinsider.com/how-resumes-have-evolved-since-their-first-creation-in-1482-2011-2

"Sectors outside of tech . . . are experiencing the same type of rapid employment needs": Gartner, 2021, "Gartner survey reveals talent shortages as biggest barrier to emerging technologies adoption," press release, September 3, https://www.gartner.com/en/newsroom/press-releases/2021-09-13-gartner-survey-reveals-talent-shortages-as-biggest-barrier-to-emerging-technologies-adoption

Caminiti, S., 2022, "Tech talent is still in demand but outsized salaries may be disappearing," CNBC, June 19, https://www.cnbc.com/2022/06/19/tech-talent-still-in-demand-but-outsized-salaries-are-disappearing.html

Chapter Five: The Future of Work

1. Provost, F. and Fawcett, T., 2013, *Data Science for Business: What You Need to Know About Data Mining and Data-analytic Thinking*, O'Reilly Media.

2. Pathak, R., 2021, "How Apple uses AI and big data," *Analytics Steps* (blog), January 20, https://www.analyticssteps.com/blogs/how-apple-uses-ai-and-big-data

   Bulygo, Z., n.d. "How Netflix uses analytics to select movies, create content, and make multimillion dollar decisions," *Neil Patel* (blog), retrieved on October 10, 2022, from, https://neilpatel.com/blog/how-netflix-uses-analytics/

   Belyh, A., 2019, "Big data and new product development," Cleverism, September 19, https://www.cleverism.com/big-data-new-product-development/

3. McDonald's Corporation, 2019, "McDonald's to acquire dynamic yield, will use dynamic technology to increase personalization and improve customer experience," press release, March 26, https://www.prnewswire.com/il/news-releases/mcdonalds-to-acquire-dynamic-yield-will-use-decision-technology-to-increase-personalization-and-improve-customer-experience-300818098.html

   Pathak, R., 2020, "How Amazon uses big data," *Analytics Steps* (blog), November 3, https://www.analyticssteps.com/blogs/how-amazon-uses-big-data

   Pastukhov, D., 2022, "Inside Spotify's recommender system: A complete guide to Spotify recommendation algorithms," *Music Tomorrow* (blog), February 9, https://www.music-tomorrow.com/blog/how-spotify-recommendation-system-works-a-complete-guide-2022

4. Jackson, J., 2019, "How Uber Eats uses machine learning to estimate delivery times," The New Stack, July 19, https://thenewstack.io/how-uber-eats-uses-machine-learning-to-estimate-delivery-times/

Impact Networking, 2021, "Big data analytics examples that can help your business," *Impact My Biz* (blog), September 16, https://www.impactmybiz.com/blog/blog-3-big-data-analytics-examples-that-can-help-your-business/

Logan, M., 2015, "The wearable prepping the US Women's Soccer Team for battle," *Wired*, June 22, https://www.wired.com/2015/06/wearable-prepping-us-womens-soccer-team-battle/

5. Asku, Hulya, 2013, "Customer service: The new proactive marketing," *Huffington Post*, March 26, https://www.huffpost.com/entry/customer-service-the-new_b_2827889

6. O'Donnell, J.T., 2016, "How your company's lame hiring process is losing you customers," *Fast Company*, April 5, https://www.fastcompany.com/3058571/how-your-companys-lame-hiring-process-is-losing-you-customers

Steiner, K., 2017, "Bad candidate experience cost Virgin Media $5M annually—Here is how they turned that around," LinkedIn, March 15, https://www.linkedin.com/business/talent/blog/talent-acquisition/bad-candidate-experience-cost-virgin-media-5m-annually-and-how-they-turned-that-around

7. TMP Worldwide, n.d., "Virgin Media—NPS *Driving the Candidate Experience*," retrieved on October 5, 2022, from https://www.tmpw.co.uk/case-study/virgin-media-net-promoter-score/

"But in the early 90s, two management consultants, Richard Fairbank"; "Fairbank and Morris saw an opportunity for bank profitability"; "They finally garnered the interest of a small Virginia-based bank"; "Signet started a credit division using this new, data-driven methodology": Provost, F. and Fawcett, T., 2013, *Data Science for Business: What You Need to Know About Data Mining and Data-analytic Thinking*, O'Reilly Media.

"Fairbank and Morris collected the standard data": Martens, D. and Provost, F., 2011, September, "Pseudo-social network targeting from consumer transaction data," NYU Working Paper No. CEDER-11-05, https://ssrn.com/abstract=1934670

Knowledge at Wharton, 2004, December 15, "When leadership becomes a quest," https://knowledge.wharton.upenn.edu/article/when-leadership-becomes-a-quest

Chapter Six: The Culture Crutch

1. Naber, A., n.d., "One third of your life is spent at work," Gettysburg College, retrieved on October 10, 2022, from https://www.gettysburg.edu/news/stories?id=79db7b34-630c-4f49-ad32-4ab9ea48e72bandpageTitle=1%2F3+of+your+life+is+spent+at+work

2. PricewaterhouseCooper, n.d., "Making work more meaningful: Building a fulfilling employee experience," retrieved on October 11, 2022, from https://d0cb2f2608c10c70e72a-fc7154704217aa017aa46150bf00c30c.ssl.cf5.rackcdn.com/pwc-building-a-fulfilling-employee-experience.pdf

3. Hastings, R., 2009, "Culture Deck," Slideshare, https://www.slideshare.net/reed2001/culture-1798664

4. Hastings, "Culture Deck."

5. Macrotrends, n.d., "Netflix: Number of employees 2010–2022," retrieved on October 11, 2022, from https://www.macrotrends.net/stocks/charts/NFLX/netflix/number-of-employees
Statistica, n.d., "Number of Netflix employees from 2015 to 2022, by type," retrieved on October 11, 2022, from https://www.statista.com/statistics/587671/netflix-employees/
Comparably, n.d., "Netflix competitors," retrieved on October 11, 2022, from https://www.comparably.com/companies/netflix/competitors
Castillo, M., 2018, "Netflix reportedly encourages execs to widely explain why they fire people," CNBC, October 25, https://www.cnbc.com/2018/10/25/netflix-transparency-encourages-execs-to-talk-about-firings.html

6. Schiffer, Z., 2022, "Netflix doesn't want to hear it anymore," The Verge, July 7, https://www.theverge.com/23196764/netflix-culture-ted-sarandos-employee-feedback-dave-chappelle-controversy

7. Baruch, Y., 2022, "Netflix offers the door to workers offended by the streaming platform's content," Yahoo! May 14, https://www.yahoo.com/video/netflix-offers-door-workers-offended-193427791.html

8. Andrews-Dyer, H., 2021, "Dave Chappelle's controversial comedy special is a catalyst for change as Netflix walkout leads to calls for reform," *Washington Post*, October 20, https://www.washingtonpost.com/arts-entertainment/2021/10/20/netflix-chappelle-controversy/

9. Hastings, R. and Meyer, E., 2020, *No Rules Rules: Netflix and the Culture of Reinvention*, Penguin.

10. Rodriguez, A., 2020, "How to get a job at Netflix," *Business Insider*, January 30, https://www.businessinsider.com/how-to-get-a-job-at-netflix-tips-guide-hr-2020-1

11. Phipps, M., 2021, "The history of pension plans in the US," The Balance, October 14, https://www.thebalancemoney.com/the-history-of-the-pension-plan-2894374
    Cornish, A., (host), 2019, "President William Howard Taft wanted all of the US to have 3 months of vacation," podcast episode of *All Things Considered*, NPR, August 1, https://www.npr.org/2019/08/01/747368652/president-william-howard-taft-wanted-all-of-the-u-s-to-have-3-months-of-vacation#
    Bucci, M., 1991, October, "Growth of employer-sponsored group life insurance," Bureau of Labor Statistics, https://www.bls.gov/opub/mlr/1991/10/art4full.pdf
    Siegel, M., 2019, "The forgotten origins of paid family leave," *New York Times*, November 29, https://www.nytimes.com/2019/11/29/opinion/mothers-paid-family-leave.html
    Kaiser Permanente, 2011, July 21, "How it all started," https://about.kaiserpermanente.org/our-story/our-history/how-it-all-started

12. Bradford, L., 2016, "13 tech companies that offer cool work perks," *Forbes*, July 27, https://www.forbes.com/sites/

laurencebradford/2016/07/27/13-tech-companies-that-offer-insanely-cool-perks/?sh=7eea320079d1

13. Bradford, "13 tech companies that offer cool work perks."

14. Acaroglu, L., n.d., "Future of the sustainable workplace in the age of COVID-19 and climate change," Unily, retrieved on October 12, 2022, from https://www.unily.com/media/x5eljtve/unily-future-of-the-sustainable-workplace-guide.pdf

15. PAWS/LA., n.d., "List of companies with matching gifts programs," retrieved on October 12, 2022, from https://www.pawsla.org/uploads/5/9/3/3/59339749/list_of_companies_with_matching_gift_programs.pdf

    Simmons, J., n.d., "Most unique environmentally friendly benefits at green companies," Monster, retrieved on October 12, 2022, from https://www.monster.com/career-advice/article/most-unique-environmentally-friendly-benefits-at-green-companies

    Timberland, n.d. "Work hard, play dirty—The Timberland Victory Garden," retrieved on October 12, 2022, from https://www.timberland.com/responsibility/stories/timberland-victory-garden.html

    Vermont Investment Energy Corp, n.d., "Our story," retrieved on October 12, 2022, from https://www.veic.org/company/story

16. Gemeš, N., 2022, "17 green companies that are good for you and the environment," *Green Citizen* (blog), June 5, https://greencitizen.com/blog/green-companies/

    Fernandes, P., 2022, "What is the triple bottom line?" Business.com, September 6, https://www.business.com/articles/triple-bottom-line-defined/

17. Global Sustainable Investment Alliance, 2021, "Global sustainable investment review 2020," http://www.gsi-alliance.org/wp-content/uploads/2021/08/GSIR-20201.pdf

18. Maurer, R., 2019, "Flexible work critical to retention, survey finds," Society for Human Resource Management, September

19, https://www.shrm.org/resourcesandtools/hr-topics/talent-acquisition/pages/flexible-work-critical-retention.aspx

19. Hubspot, n.d., "Benefits & perks," retrieved on October 12, 2022, from https://www.hubspot.com/careers/benefits

Vistaprint, n.d., "Work where you work best," retrieved on October 12, 2022, from https://careers.vista.com/remote-first/

Kelly, J., 2022, "Twitter employees can work from home 'forever' or 'wherever you feel most productive and creative,'" *Forbes*, March 5, https://www.forbes.com/sites/jackkelly/2022/03/05/twitter-employees-can-work-from-home-forever-or-wherever-you-feel-most-productive-and-creative

20. Figueroa, A., 2012, "Chobani founder turns centuries old Greek yogurt into billion dollar craze," NBC News, December 12, https://www.nbcnews.com/nightly-news/chobani-founder-turns-centuries-old-greek-yogurt-billion-dollar-craze-flna1c7580650

Ferdman, R., 2015, "Goodbye, good old Greek yogurt," *Washington Post*, December 18, https://www.washingtonpost.com/news/wonk/wp/2015/12/18/goodbye-good-old-greek-yogurt/

"Back then, fringe benefits consisted of paid vacations": Chen, Y. P., 1981, "The growth of fringe benefits: implications for social security," Bureau of Labor Statistics, November, https://www.bls.gov/opub/mlr/1981/11/art1full.pdf

Turner, R., n.d., "Fringe benefits," Colgate University, retrieved on October 14, 2022, from https://www.urban.org/sites/default/files/publication/71096/1000532-Fringe-Benefits.PDF

The Hartford, 2020, August 4, "From fringe to forefront: The genesis story of fringe benefits," https://www.thehartford.com/insights/employee-benefits/fringe-benefits

"In this group of eight": "Traitorous eight," 2022, *Wikipedia,* October 18, https://en.wikipedia.org/w/index.php?title=Traitorous_eightandoldid=1094731828

"Massive machines powered by vacuum tubes were state of the art": "ENIAC" 2022, *Wikipedia,* October 18, https://en. wikipedia.org/w/index.php?title=ENIACandoldid=1116018553

Chapter Seven: A Human-Centric Workforce

1. Ingraham, N., 2012, "Best Buy posts $1.7 billion quarterly loss due to restructuring costs, plans to close 50 stores," The Verge, March 29, https://www.theverge.com/2012/3/29/2910547/best-buy-q4-2012-financials-50-US-store-closures
   Hsu, T., 2012, "Best Buy profit tanks 91%, stock tumbles to 9-year low," *Los Angeles Times,* August 21, https://www.latimes.com/business/la-xpm-2012-aug-21-la-fi-mo-best-buy-earnings-2012 0821-story.html
   Berfield, S. and Boyle, M., 2018, "Best Buy should be dead, but it's thriving in the age of Amazon," Bloomberg, July 19, https://www.bloomberg.com/news/features/2018-07-19/best-buy-should-be-dead-but-it-s-thriving-in-the-age-of-amazon
2. Adegoke, Y., 2008, "Best Buy to buy Napster for $121 million," Reuters, September 15, https://www.reuters.com/article/us-napster-bestbuy/best-buy-to-buy-napster-for-121-million-idUSN 1550308820080915
   Carucci, R., 2021, "Behind the scenes of Best Buy's record-setting turnaround with Hubert Joly," *Forbes,* April 4, https://www.forbes.com/sites/roncarucci/2021/04/04/behind-the-scenes-of-best-buys-record-setting-turnaround-with-hubert-joly/?sh=65591 f1853f0
3. Business Travel News, 2010, "Joly as one of the 25 most influential executives of the business travel industry 2006 and 2009," *Business Travel News Magazine,* January 25.
4. Gelles, D., 2021, "Hubert Joly turned Best Buy around. Now he's trying to fix capitalism," *New York Times,* July 15, https://www.nytimes.com/2021/07/15/business/hubert-joly-corner-office-best-buy.html

5. Carucci, "Behind the scenes of Best Buy's record-setting turnaround."

6. Occupational Health and Safety Administration, n.d., "The Triangle Shirtwaist Factory Fire," https://www.osha.gov/aboutosha/40-years/trianglefactoryfire
Boissoneault, L., 2017, "The coal mining massacre America forgot," *Smithsonian Magazine*, April 25, https://www.smithsonianmag.com/history/forgotten-matewan-massacre-was-epicenter-20th-century-mine-wars-180963026/

7. Kwan, A., Neveras, N., Schwartz, J., Pelster, B., Erickson, R., and Szpaichler, S., 2020, *Talent 2020: Surveying the Talent Paradox from the Employee Perspective*, Deloitte University Press, https://www2.deloitte.com/content/dam/Deloitte/mx/Documents/about-deloitte/Talent2020_Employee-Perspective.pdf

8. Stillman, J., 2012, "Your perks aren't motivating your employees," *Inc.*, February 20, https://www.inc.com/jessica-stillman/why-your-perks-are-not-motivating-your-employees.html

9. Gallup, 2022, "State of the global workplace: 2022 report," https://www.gallup.com/workplace/349484/state-of-the-global-workplace.aspx

10. Gallup, "State of the global workplace: 2022 report."
Achor, S., 2018, *Big Potential: How Transforming the Pursuit of Success Raises Our Achievement, Happiness and Well-being*, Currency.

11. Greene, J., 2015, "10 years later, Amazon celebrates Prime's triumph," *Seattle Times*, February 2, https://www.seattletimes.com/business/amazon/10-years-later-amazon-celebrates-primes-triumph/
Fahey, R., 2007, "Farewell, Father," Eurogamer, April 30, https://www.eurogamer.net/farewell-father-article
Gohil, P., 2020, "A story on how Apple got the idea of 'Slide to Unlock,'" LinkedIn, July 21, https://www.linkedin.com/pulse/story-how-apple-got-idea-slide-unlock-parth-gohil/
Xerox, n.d., "Xerox history timeline," retrieved on October 12, 2022, from https://www.xerox.com/en-us/about/history-timeline

12. Scholly, 2021, April 22, "50 Companies with amazing tuition reimbursement programs," https://myscholly.com/50-companies-with-amazing-tuition-reimbursement-programs/

    Intel Corporation, 2022, "Intel rewards experience," recruiting brochure, https://www.intel.com/content/dam/www/central-libraries/us/en/documents/us-rewards-recruiting-brochure-2022.pdf

13. Girls Who Code, 2021, "Annual report 2021," https://girlswhocode.com/2021report/

14. Konstantinides, A., 2020, "Ina Garten says she quit her White House job to buy a grocery shop at the age of 30 thanks to advice from her husband," *Insider*, October 21, https://www.insider.com/ina-garten-left-white-house-job-became-famous-cook-2020-10

    Mellor, W., Chen, L.Y., and Wu, Z., 2014, "How the tech-unsavvy Jack Ma took Alibaba public and became China's richest man," *Washington Post*, November 22, https://www.washingtonpost.com/business/how-the-tech-unsavvy-jack-ma-took-alibaba-public-and-became-chinas-richest-man/2014/11/20/234ed758-6e8c-11e4-ad12-3734c461eab6_story.html

    Liu, J., 2019, "How to change careers, according to 50 people who made a pivot," *Forbes*, April 2, https://www.forbes.com/sites/josephliu/2019/04/02/successfully-change-careers/?sh=662c2c21525c

    Biography.com, 2014, April 2, "Ray Kroc biography," https://www.biography.com/business-figure/ray-kroc

15. Cameron, L., n.d., "How a woman named 'Steve' became one of Britain's most celebrated IT pioneers, entrepreneurs, and philanthropists," *IEEE Computer Society*, retrieved on October 15, 2022, from https://www.computer.org/publications/tech-news/research/dame-stephanie-steve-shirley-computer-pioneer

16. Shirley, S. 2012, *Let IT Go*, UK: Lightning Source UK.

    Dame Shirley, n.d., "Philanthropy," retrieved on October 15, 2022, from https://www.steveshirley.com/philanthropy/

Shirley, S. and Reed, A., 2019, "The Shirley Foundation spend out," *Philanthropy Impact*, June, https://www.philanthropy-impact.org/resource/shirley-foundation-spend-out

17. Akris, n.d., "A woman with purpose: Dame Stephanie Shirley," *Akris* (blog), retrieved on October 12, 2022, from https://us.akris.com/blogs/women-with-purpose/a-woman-with-purpose-dame-stephanie-shirley

"In retrospect we can see that Joly was, for lack of a better phrase, a man of the people": Gelles, D., 2021, "Hubert Joly turned Best Buy around. Now he's trying to fix capitalism," *New York Times*, July 15, https://www.nytimes.com/2021/07/15/business/hubert-joly-corner-office-best-buy.html

Roose, K., 2017, "Best Buy's secrets for thriving in the Amazon age," *New York Times*, September 18, https://www.nytimes.com/2017/09/18/business/best-buy-amazon.html

"Next was building genuine human connections": Reiss, R., 2021, "Former Best Buy CEO Hubert Joly shares the secrets to company turnaround," *Forbes*, April 20, https://www.forbes.com/sites/robertreiss/2021/04/20/former-best-buy-ceo-hubert-joly-shares-the-secret-to-company-turnarounds

"For example, at a Best Buy in Florida, a young mother came in with her son": McLellan, S., 2019, "Best Buy employees perform 'surgery' on 3-year-old's beloved toy dinosaur," *Good Morning America*, March 5, https://www.goodmorningamerica.com/family/story/best-buy-employees-perform-surgery-year-olds-beloved-61389519

"After World War II, greater harmony emerged as labor reforms"; "That was a central tenet of employee value through the late 1980s": Georgetown University Law Center, 2010, "A timeline of the evolution of retirement in the United States," https://scholarship.law.georgetown.edu/legal/50

"'Workaholism' was prevalent": Klein, E., (host), 2021, "The case against loving your job," podcast episode of *The Ezra Klein*

Show, November 9, *New York Times,* https://podcasts.apple.com/us/podcast/the-case-against-loving-your-job/id1548604447?i=1000542446662

"EVPs have long been managed by the same three principles": Venkataramani, S., 2021, "Make way for a more human-centric employee value proposition," Gartner, May 13, https://www.gartner.com/smarterwithgartner/make-way-for-a-more-human-centric-employee-value-proposition

The Conference Board, 2020, June 30, "DNA of engagement: How organizations can align engagement and inclusion to enhance employee experience," https://www.conference-board.org/topics/dna-of-engagement/how-organizations-can-align-engagement-inclusion

"When Richard Montañez got a job as a janitor at Frito-Lay": Montañez, R., 2021, *Flamin' Hot: The Incredible True Story of One Man's Rise from Janitor to Top Executive,* Penguin Random House Canada, https://www.penguinrandomhouse.ca/books/622527/flamin-hot-by-richard-montanez/9780593087466

"That's what happened to Reshma Saujani": Faduly, L., 2018, "Not everyone can afford a job they love," *The Atlantic,* July 17, https://www.theatlantic.com/technology/archive/2018/07/reshma-saujani-girls-who-code/562055/

"Consider the story of Building 20": Hilts, P. J., 1998, "Last rites for a 'Plywood Palace' that was a rock of science," *New York Times,* March 31, https://www.nytimes.com/1998/03/31/science/last-rites-for-a-plywood-palace-that-was-a-rock-of-science.html

Penfield, P., Jr., 1997, December 19, "MIT's building 20: The magical incubator 1943–1998," MIT Department of Electrical Engineering and Computer Science, retrieved and archived at https://web.archive.org/web/20080723202157/http://www.eecs.mit.edu/building/20/

Lehrer, J., 2012, "Groupthink," *New Yorker,* January 22, https://www.newyorker.com/magazine/2012/01/30/groupthink

"When Dame Stephanie Shirley was five years old": Shirley, S., 2015, "Why do ambitious women have flat heads?" Video, Ted Conferences, https://www.ted.com/talks/dame_stephanie_shirley_why_do_ambitious_women_have_flat_heads/

Index